Love Notes from the Soul 2.0
STORIES OF HEALING + COMPASSION

CYNTHIA GREGORY, EDITOR

Love Notes from the Soul 2.0
© 2025 Cynthia Gregory
Maycamas Press

All rights reserved. This book, or any portion thereof may not be reproduced or used in any manner whatsoever without the express written permission of the publisher, except for the use of brief quotations in a book review.

Edited by: Cynthia Gregory / Nora Joanne Gerber
Cover & interior: Mariah Miller Creative Services

ISBN Registration:
Tradepaper: 978-1-7375749-5-8
Digital: 978-1-7375749-4-1

SPECIAL NOTES

All LOVE NOTES stories are original and authentic intellectual property of their authors. The following previously published excerpts have been granted permission to appear in this book.

"Birthing the Wild Feminine" was excerpted from *Awakening the Divine Feminine: Stories of Healing, Inspiration, and Empowerment* (2025)

"Evolution Revolution" was excerpted from the book *Evolution Revolution* (2025)

"I Donated My Breast Milk and Found My Faith" was excerpted from *Lilith Magazine* (March 2025)

"Overwhelming Peace" was excerpted from *Bring Forth Soul Consciousness* (2023)

FOREWORD

I have it on good authority that one must BELIEVE a book into being. From the start, LOVE NOTES 2.0 was a book that insisted on being. Actually, the essence of the book, if you can call it that, demanded it. Once launched, the LOVE NOTES project began to exert a gravitational pull of its own, calling in soulful creatives whose wisdom and light were so unmistakable as to be written in neon above their heads. Some stories appeared instantly. Some stories evolved like caterpillars into butterflies. I learned, in the process of stewarding this second edition of LOVE NOTES, that the creative spark, multiplied by a chorus of voices united in vision, evolves with grace.

The title LOVE NOTES may suggest light reading, but these stories require something from the reader. They share intimacies with outrageous courage and sparkling generosity. They explore the territories of love and family and belonging and resilience. They honor the journeys of seekers and refugees, of warriors, and of our better angels. In short, they elevate compassion to an art form. Baring your soul in a room (or book) full of strangers is an exercise in power and vulnerability that brokers peace and fosters understanding. In order to do this well, you must know what it means to be flawed and human and perfect. These authors are some of the bravest people I know, but I'm not sure they would agree. They would say that they're just doing what's right. Or doing what's fair. Or exercising good judgment or kindness. You see where I'm going with this. Those who share their deepest secrets give us all courage to do the same.

It is, of course, possible to experience these literary lucid dreams passively, but by engaging heart, mind, and soul, readers may find themselves transported to another realm altogether. The combined frequencies of these shared stories exude a charm that can elevate the reader to a deeper level of understanding of our beautiful, complex, and sometimes terrifying world. They remind us of what a miracle life is when we allow it to be.

These twenty-seven LOVE NOTES from the Soul are iconic. They are zesty and chewy and picante in deliciously reverent ways. All on their own, they shine a light on the everyday sacred ... and as a body of collected wisdom, they amplify it. They require the reader to engage hope, love, kindness, courage, or any aspect of generosity one might name. This book does not promise to be an easy read, but it does promise to inspire the mind, expand the heart, and seduce the soul in such a way as to leave an imprint. We are glad you are here.

Cynthia Gregory
Editor and Curator

TABLE OF CONTENTS

1. ALIGNED IN LOVE + BEYOND....................1
   Russ and Sunny Watts

2. LOVE IS ALWAYS THE ANSWER....................9
   DeAnna Pursai

3. COURAGE AND SERVICE........................17
   Dee Dee Kiesow

4. DOG + PONY SHOW 25
   Catherine Kaufer

5. BECAUSE PETS ARE FAMILY....................33
   Anna M. van Heeckeren, DVM, MS

6. THE DESK MOMENT:...........................41
   Redefining Success on My Own Terms
   Sarah Olivieri, MPS

7. THE BEST DAY OF MY LIFE 49
   Brandon Peacock

8. MY LOVE LETTER TO DRUMMING:................55
   Journeys of Rhythm, Courage, and Community
   Lorenzo Jones

9. LEARNING TO LOVE WORDS AGAIN 63
   Deana Kitajima

10. BORN FOR BLISS 71
    Lisa Martin Naimi

11. SAINT TOBIAS: A Love that Bridges All 79
    Dawn Airhart Witte

12. FEROCIOUS COMPASSION 85
    Sandra Bargman

13. BIRTHING THE WILD FEMININE WITHIN..........93
    Esther Wyss-Flamm

14. HOW I LET GO OF MY BREASTMILK & FOUND FAITH... 101
    Leah Kahn

15. MAKING MEDICINE FROM GRIEF: 107
    A Story of Stillness, Suffering, and Surrender to Motion
    Jennifer Coffey

16. SOUL NOTES 115
    Sheherazad Barnes

17. THE POWER OF PERCEPTION 123
    Lilly Melgar

18. LOVE + RELEASE 129
    Tracey Rose

19. ALL DADS MATTER 137
    Ana Mercedes Rivera-Pagan

20. FROM MEAGER MEANS TO BEING ALL THAT! 145
    Viera Whye

21. LOGGED IN AND CHECKED OUT 153
    Ceara Fate

22. A LEGACY OF SERVICE 159
    Leonard Weingarten

23. CULTIVATING COMPASSION 167
    Ken Harootunian

24. RIDING THE DRAGON 175
    Yukiko Amaya

25. OVERWHELMING PEACE 185
    Rev. Annie Bachelder

26. ME AND MAGDALENA: Healing Holy Heretics 191
    Shelley Lynn Hines, MSN

27. HUMANITY'S DESTINY 197
    Zaher Kury

ABOUT OUR AUTHORS 201

ACKNOWLEDGEMENTS 231

For cultural creatives everywhere whose soul-deep story was ever minimized, who were told they were too vivacious, too radiant, too incandescent, too audacious, too much for a world not yet ready to receive them. For the dreamers whose visions were deemed too willful, too majestic, too expansive to fit within the narrow bounds of convention. For those whose hearts ache to connect with something grander: a higher calling, a deeper exploration, a song that calls to them to live boldly and share their authentic wisdom. May they discover that by courageously revealing their own journey of love, insight, and transformation, they grant others the permission to do the same.

1
ALIGNED IN LOVE + BEYOND

Russ and Sunny Watts

The story of how we came to be WE sometimes feels too good to be true. But it's both too good and too true.

Sunny: I was teaching in Washington, DC, and I had to move out of the place where I was living, as it had become infested with mold. And so I wrote an email to my work community and said, '*Hey, if anybody knows of anything that'd be great, I would love to continue to walk to work,*' because I lived a block away.

One of my colleagues sent back three different possibilities that he knew of. The first one was a basement apartment like I had been renting. I looked at it, but the owner just creeped me out, and it didn't feel right.

I looked at the second apartment, which had a little garden. It was furnished so that helped but it smelled kind of moldy and stale, and I had just come from that, and somebody had looked at it before me, and they had wanted it. So I didn't have to tell this sweet woman no.

The third house was a house share a few blocks from the school in this quaint little neighborhood called Foxhall Village, in Washington, DC. And I sent the landlord an email to meet up during lunch. I went for our appointment, but the landlord was a no-show. I met a cat outside who I assumed belonged to the house. The cat, Max, was sweet.

When I got back to my office, I sent an email and said, '*Hey, were we supposed to meet today?*' He wrote back, saying, '*Oh, right, I am so sorry. Let's meet tomorrow during lunch.*'

Russ: I felt so bad that I missed the first meeting with this person named Sunny. In my defense, when I was working at Georgetown, the days would start at eight in the morning, and they would just turn into six in the afternoon in a flash. And so the day that I missed my appointment with Sunny, I was truly gutted. When I say I'm going to do something, I do something, and I blew it.

So, the next day, I'm coming around the corner between my house and the Tudor-style place next door, and to my surprise, this gorgeous woman is standing between the steps from the sidewalk to the house, and I have this reaction that shivers in my bones, not just on my skin. *Dear God (whom I never spoke to)*, I thought. *Please let her live with me.* I felt like I had lost all my words.

"Hi!" I managed. "I'm so sorry. My name is Russ. Please come and see the house."

I showed her the house, and my words were, "This is our house. If you don't like the furniture, we can change it. If you don't like the paint, we can paint it. If you want to have a party, you can have a party. You don't have to ask me. This is your house. It's not a house that you're sharing with the landlord. I don't want you to feel like you're living in my house. It's our house."

I gave her a tour of the entire house. Somewhere around there, she met Max again, and probably Leo and Tatiana—the three cats.

Later that day, I got a message from Sunny saying, *Yes, I'd like to live in your house*, and I think I did the biggest, longest, happy dance of my life. She moved in a few days later. It just so happens that that weekend was already planned with my Executive Master's in Leadership program at Georgetown. All of my colleagues showed up at the house, and Sunny was there too, and we basically slid into the process of "now we're hosts together."

Sunny: As the party started, I was in my room, texting with Christine, my dearest girlfriend. She said I should go. I hesitated—I didn't know anyone there.

"What music is playing?" she asked.

"Country," I said.

"Alright, well, he gets a demerit for that."

I averred, "Yeah, but he's really cute, so maybe it balances out."

Russ: Meanwhile, my grad school colleagues were curious—I'd been showing up stag everywhere, and suddenly I had this fetching new housemate. They came over to meet her. Technically, I did have a girlfriend at the time, and she had a boyfriend. Neither of them was at the party.

During the party, we were cleaning up in the kitchen. She was at the sink, and I told her to leave the dishes, touching her hip ever so slightly. In my head, I was thinking, '*Oh my God, we're hosting; this feels so great.*'

Sunny: That was the first inclination that there was a magnetism at play. After that, we got into the groove of living together, both busy with work. Sometimes we'd be home at the same time, cook together, share wine, and suddenly it would be three in the morning, still sitting on the kitchen floor talking. We lost track of time many times.

In October, Russ was gone for three weeks running the Colorado River. He left the keys with his ex-wife, Costanza, who came to feed the cats. During that time, I got to meet her—she was lovely. It was probably better that I met her as Russ's housemate rather than his girlfriend because she can be protective, and this way we met without any tension. We talked about him a lot, getting an inside scoop.

He sent me a necklace from Colorado, just as a thank-you for being his housemate. When he got back, we had a few more evenings together. Later, around Thanksgiving, I went to London to meet a possible romantic interest—which didn't work out—and Russ picked me up from the airport. We unloaded a truck full of wood from his best friend's family farm together. We were doing more things together. Since we both loved climbing, we decided to go climbing. It was a certified "non-date date" since we were both seeing other people. We had two of those non-dates—climbing, then crepes at a French bistro in Georgetown.

One day, my best friend at work and I decided to go away and travel during the holidays. We decided that Athens seemed like a fun (and warm) destination. I told Russ, and he mentioned that Athens wouldn't be that warm—but that he was going to Fiji.

"Do you want to come?" he asked.

I told Julia, and she immediately said yes. Soon, we were buying tickets, leaving December 26, returning just in time to start school again in January. When I realized how expensive it was to fly from DC to LAX to Nadi, Fiji, I had second thoughts. Money was tight for me—I was living on a teaching salary. Julia looked me in the eyes, grabbed my shoulders, shook me, and said, "Sunny, this is your future husband. Leave money out of the equation!" I laughed and bought the ticket.

Russ had been quietly hoping it would be just the two of us, but when I said "we" were coming, he recalibrated. Still, traveling to Fiji with two beautiful women wasn't a bad thing.

On December 26, I had a ten-hour layover in LA, so I spent the time with Russ's sister and nieces. We played Wii and laughed a lot. We landed in Fiji on his birthday, and Julia immediately bought us rum drinks for breakfast. We also stocked up on food, candy, school supplies, and medical supplies for the village we were visiting.

The chief of the village picked us up by boat—no roads there, only a hundred-meter stretch from the airport to the dock. We spent our first night at the chief's home, sleeping on woven mats after a traditional kava ceremony.

The next day, we kayaked a few hours to stay at a tiny one-room structure with a lofted bed, a futon on the floor, mosquito nets, and an outdoor kerosene stove. From there, we kayaked out to Vesi Beach and hung out.

That night, Russ cooked a three-course meal: curry, rice, and pudding. We shared Bundaberg rum under a sky full of stars, no light pollution, no electricity. Julia, tipsy and persistent, kept asking each of us if we liked the other, if we would kiss. Eventually, she passed out, starfished on the double bed under her mosquito net.

We tucked her in, then looked at the single bed left. "Should we make our bed?" we asked. We brushed our teeth, lay down next to each other for the first time, and had our first kiss.

The rest of the trip was magical: bioluminescent kayaking at night, laughter with village kids, intimacy that felt like a dream. When I thought of returning to DC, nothing in our "real life" had changed—yet the connection was undeniable. Nothing and everything had changed. I caught myself thinking/praying again, *Dear Whomever, please let this be, let this stick, after we get home.*

When we got back from Fiji, it was clear: we were no longer just housemates. We moved into the same room. The first night, we were surrounded by moving boxes and laundry baskets, but we both felt it—the shift from "you" and "me" to "us." The Fiji magic had followed us home.

Russ: It was January in DC—cold, gray, the kind of weather that makes you nostalgic for tropical beaches. We tried to slip back into "normal life," but it was impossible. At first, we were still technically in those other relationships. But they faded quickly. There were more late-night kitchen conversations, cooking side by side, laughing until we cried. Sometimes we'd be talking and realize hours had passed, the candles burned down, the wine glasses empty.

On February 27, just a couple of days past Sunny's birthday, I woke up, and I felt in my soul, *you must ask her now to marry you—NOW*. So I turned to her and said, "Will you take my hand in this journey?" And she said yes.

Sunny: We were married at the courthouse two weeks later, with my parents and our two best friends by our side.

Three months later, we had a 10-day celebration in the Adirondack Mountains. There was a big party on the first Saturday, exactly three months after we were married, complete with dear friends from across the globe, food, drinks, dancing, and a beautiful ceremony that we created with those we love and who love us in return.

We chose to have a long celebration so that we could actually spend time with the people we enjoy, instead of the traditional wedding that is over too fast, never enough time to even speak to everyone in a meaningful way. This way, we could hike, play, cook, hang out, and truly enjoy the company around us.

And here we are now—still partners in every sense, still talking late into the night, still cooking side by side, still saying "yes" to the adventures that call us.

When people ask about our story now, we laugh because it feels like the universe conspired to put us in the same house—and then kept giving us reasons to stay in each other's orbit until we couldn't imagine leaving.

Living together from the very beginning meant we had to navigate daily life right away—bills, groceries, laundry, moods, and messes.

There was no "honeymoon phase" in the traditional sense. Our love was built in the trenches of real life, which is why it feels so grounded.

Over the years, we've realized that what drew us to each other wasn't just chemistry. It was alignment. We both want to live in ways that make the world more equitable, more compassionate, and more connected. We believe in lifting others up, especially those whose voices are often silenced. We believe in listening deeply and acting with intention.

That's why so much of our life together has revolved around service. Whether it's through Russ's leadership work or my community projects, we see our marriage as a partnership in purpose. We show up for each other so we can show up for others.

We've learned that compassion starts at home—in how we speak to each other, how we resolve conflict, and how we celebrate wins. If we can't live our values with each other, we can't authentically offer them to the world.

Our vision is simple: a life full of love, curiosity, and generosity. A life that says "yes" to connection and "no" to fear. A life that keeps inviting people in, the way we did on that first night as accidental co-hosts of a party neither of us planned together.

The details of our story—the moldy apartment, the missed meeting, the cats, the rum drinks in Fiji—are just the setting. The real story is about choosing each other, again and again, and choosing to make our partnership a platform for kindness.

Fifteen years later, with two beautiful kids, we still talk late into the night. We still cook side by side. And we still believe that a shared life, lived with purpose, can ripple outward in ways we may never fully see—but will always trust we are making the world a little better.

Russ: I had a dream. I got my dream, and I'm sharing it. I'm giving my kids a slice of the dream, and sometimes I imagine how that ripples into the world. That's the beauty of the butterfly effect. And yet I don't propose that our life's adventure has to change anybody's life except ours, our children, and our close family.

One of our goals as parents is to help our children understand that they're citizens of the world. When people meet our kids, they're like, "Gosh—they sail, they travel, they're so curious and inquisitive! What cool humans they are."

It's an honor to be part of this beautiful life.

2
LOVE IS ALWAYS THE ANSWER

DeAnna Pursai

There's a popular saying: *Regardless of the question, Love is always the answer.* As I've gotten older, over time, I realize how much I resonate with this saying and how much I strive to live by this truth on my life path.

One of the true loves of my life is my sister. My sister's name is Angel, and she's roughly a year-and-a-half my junior. She is brilliant, funny, kind, bright, entertaining, and purely joyful. She also happens to have Down syndrome.

My mother tells the story of Angel, who was born on a warm summer morning in rural Indiana in 1973. She was immediately whisked out of the delivery room. Roughly ten minutes later, the doctor came solemnly back to inform my parents that their baby would never be able to walk, talk, clothe, or feed herself. He asserted his professional recommendation was that she be immediately placed in an institution.

The doctor could not have appreciated the fierce spirit of my mother, Jill. "Bring me my baby," she demanded. Later, my mother confided to me that she knew full well there was no way clinicians could have conducted any valid tests in such a short time.

Fearing the worst of extreme physical deformities, my mother recollected that when a warm, pink bundle was deposited into her arms, she counted ten soft fingers and toes. She then looked the doctor squarely in the eye and declared, "Thanks, but no thanks. I'll be taking my baby home."

Angel did indeed learn how to walk, talk, clothe, and feed herself, and she became an integral and beloved member of our family. As a family, we would often joke, "Boy, did the doctor get it wrong about the talking part." Honestly, Angel has such a gift for gab that our challenge is very much figuring out how to get her to stop!

As close sisters, we had a rich and joyful childhood growing up joined at the hip in Bluffton, Indiana. My mom took Angel everywhere, included her in everything my brother and I did, and she was hands-down my forever play and soulmate.

Angel had a natural and acute sense of comedic timing and wit. She could walk into a room, read the room, and know just what to say to get a laugh out of folks. Mom shared about the time she took nearly teenage Angel to the Wednesday evening Bible study class at church. At the end of the class, each person got to go around and say an individual prayer. When it was Angel's turn, my mom reported that she waited until the room got nice and quiet, placed her hands in the praying position, and declared, "Dear Lord, please help my mom stop cussing."

Over time, I began to experience this juxtaposition of how Angel behaved and functioned within our home, and how she acted out in public in front of certain groups or individuals. At times, I was utterly baffled when she refused to take action or complete tasks that I knew well she was perfectly capable of performing—like talking or holding a conversation while doing basic tasks that others were doing—such as eating at a restaurant.

As I drilled down more into these behaviors, I realized that if she was not treated with dignity or respect, or if she perceived people felt sorry for her or were condescending to her, Angel simply refused to respond. This was absolutely maddening to observe, because it felt like a self-fulfilling prophecy playing out in slow motion before me. I saw time and again how people would pity her or talk down to her. She would sense their tone and would refuse to answer or engage. Then, observing the stranger's body language, I could tell that their pity or lack of expectations became even stronger as she refused to engage. It was utter madness.

When I left for college at Purdue University, I returned home one summer to find Angel actively engaged in a work program through her post-secondary school. Her job was to clean desks at our local schools over the summer. She seemed happy and engaged. A few years later, in stark contrast, I distinctly remember visiting home, and Angel had almost doubled her body weight because she was mainly sitting at home watching a whole lot of TV and eating a whole lot of snacks.

I learned that the work program had lost its funding, and Angel had no interest in attending the only day program available, which was shared across two rural counties, and I could understand why. Angel felt bullied there by the same individuals that she had gone to school with since kindergarten. I remember making Angel her own set of business cards to run a business in pet-sitting and plant-watering. I don't believe that endeavor ever gained much traction outside our family connections.

Fast forward to 2009, and I had co-founded a college for adults with intellectual disabilities who historically have not had access to college education. Think Special Olympics in the area of lifelong learning—where you're not judged by the end-goal on the number of baskets you make or how fast you run, but by celebrating the journey of doing something together with other people that you love.

The College of Adaptive Arts (CAA) was conceived from the idea that there must be more viable and authentic options for special needs adults beyond the day program model. Day programs serve an essential role for some adults who need more supervised and direct care throughout the day, but for other adults, it can feel stale, stifling, and existential.

I discovered, along with CAA co-founder Pamela Lindsay, PhD, that for many adults mandated out of the special education post-secondary programs at age twenty-two, the landscape of potential supported options is so significantly reduced that they all but disappear. This is also the same developmental period in these young adults' lives when they are just beginning to hit their stride and realize they can and want to become a part of the larger community.

The College of Adaptive Arts officially launched in the summer of 2009 as we rented space during the day at a local dance studio in South San Jose. Our guiding light principle has always been to listen to the students and families, give it a try, and pivot and adapt accordingly. We wanted to build a model around choice, giving adults the ability to choose their college classes based on their interests and passions. Our intention was to offer a 'typical' age-appropriate college experience. We based our classes on the semester system, offering each class once a week. In those early years, Dr. Pam and I were the primary professors of most of the classes we offered.

CAA began with one musical theatre class and twelve adults. Very early on, we added classes in adaptive guitar, dance, art, and songwriting, classes that were engaging and accessible to our adult students. We continually grew our enrollment each semester from twenty-five students that first year, increasing annually at about 15–20 percent in those early years. After the dance studio, we rented a pod of rooms in a closed elementary classroom for two years. This gave us an anchor site to grow, expand, and offer more college classes, such as on-camera acting, songwriting, puppetry, and watercolor arts.

We also began implementing monthly Networking Lounge Nights for students and families who were not enrolled in the same classes, so that they could meet each other in a social environment. This soon became a tradition. I fondly remember that one of those themed nights was the Michael Jackson Night, where we brought the house down and rocked out to "Thriller" and "Beat It" with all of our one-gloved grooving! There must have been over twenty MJs there that evening, dancing to their hearts' delight!

In 2012, we lost our site because the new landlord tripled our rent overnight. We were on the go again, truly not knowing what the landscape would look like for CAA. Our student intake and business meetings were held in a local diner near our home in South San Jose. By that time, our student enrollment was roughly forty-five adult students. For the next two years, we held our CAA college classes around the community in seven wonderful venues that opened their doors to us, including the Silver Creek Sportsplex, Hope Services, and Trinity Episcopal Cathedral in downtown San Jose. I remember distinctly thinking soon after we lost that site, "Well, this has been a good run. I'm not sure that we can sustain this without another anchor location."

From 2012 to 2014, CAA offered classes around town in seven distinct locations, and our student enrollment grew to 65 students. It was then that I sensed we were really on to something special. Somehow, a spark had been ignited. We brought on some wonderful part-time staff—many with disabilities—to help teach classes. We expanded our course offerings to include cheerleading, poetry, speaking with confidence, and added a Saturday golf team and an Annual Golf Classic.

In 2014, the remarkable Case Swenson, a local businessman and Bay Area development leader, met one of our CAA cheerleaders. He was so impressed with our work that he gave us space in downtown San Jose for pennies on the dollar. This was a pure blessing to have an anchor site in a central area of San Jose next to public transit. Case's visionary generosity gave us an incubator that lasted six beautiful and productive years.

Our course offerings steadily increased during these transformative years. We expanded and diversified, adding courses in American Sign Language (ASL), Spanish, Stop Motion Animation, and Shakespeare. In 2015, our board made a critical decision that helped shape the trajectory and value proposition of the College of Adaptive Arts. Conceptually, we started forming distinct schools of study, positioning CAA as more of a community college full liberal arts establishment, rather than a traditional arts conservatory. This helped CAA establish credibility with its course offerings as a credible alternative to the traditional community college model that had not been accessible to our population of adults. We began segmenting our classes into a course catalog distinguished by the various schools, now including Schools of Communications and Health and Wellness, beyond the original fine arts offerings in music, theater, and dance. We shifted from semesters to a quarter system to continue to diversify our course offerings, giving more variety and flexible course options for our students.

In July 2020, the College of Adaptive Arts formally partnered with West Valley College in Saratoga, CA, offering an expanded layer of higher education for adults who historically have not had access. CAA is its own independent .org charity, leasing space on a beautiful college campus, and each day we strive to build more inclusive collegiate partnerships with West Valley College. West Valley College students, such as the Democracy Institute students, are able to fulfill their service-learning hours with our adult students right on their college campus!

We've secured some county and state funds to build out a workforce development program, particularly focusing on smaller, gig work opportunities. This shift enables CAA to rethink the traditional "routine" route in employment to better align with our students' passions, skills, and interests. This coursework includes future positions in Accessible Technology & Quality Control, Associate professors, Social media and marketing, and as event planners.

More than half of our staff have self-identified disabilities. Our intention is to make CAA the gold standard in demonstrating and sharing how to optimally support and cultivate a thriving neurodivergent workforce. These professionals represent the best, most hardworking and dedicated professors, staff, and faculty I've ever had the privilege of working with. They work tirelessly behind the scenes to set the CAA students and each other up for optimal success in the classroom and as viable, vibrant world citizens. The diversity of our staff truly makes CAA a special culture to work in.

We're also partnering with the West Valley College Disability and Education Support program to bring in dynamic and vibrant national thought leaders through a speaker series, such as Haben Girma, the first student to graduate from Harvard Law School who happens to be deaf-blind. CAA's vision is to become as globally available, accessible, and robust in the area of education and liberal arts as the Special Olympics is with sports and athletics.

CAA is now fifteen years strong and has operationally grown by more than three thousand percent. The vision is to position expanded lifelong higher education for adults with intellectual and developmental disabilities on every campus of higher learning around the world. This will allow the last segment of adults to truly be able to access authentic adaptive collegiate education to become successful, contributing citizens in the community.

Throughout the journey, Angel has been my co-pilot each step of the way. She participated in CAA classes in person, such as dance and poetry, when she visited me in California, and virtual classes, such as art from our family home in Indiana. She has always helped and guided me to shape and structure what is possible. I have always known in my heart that she is the smarter of the two of us. Had she not had a disability, she could have absolutely thrived in this world that is presently not optimally structured to set her up for success.

We have seen firsthand how our students thrive from an inclusive, adaptive education. I advocate for investments in new disability education legislation to create a fiscally sustainable path, enabling this model to be implemented on every campus of higher learning around the world.

Angel has incredible wisdom, insight, and intellect that have been so often overlooked in the neurotypical space. I've been privileged to have a personal Zen master in my life who has helped me continually recalibrate what is truly important in life. It certainly has not been easy, considering the many complexities of supporting a loved one with a disability. It has been no greater honor to serve her and these adults whose time has come to show the world what is possible when they're given a fair and fighting chance to showcase their abilities!

I truly believe that Love is the Answer to this life.

3

COURAGE AND SERVICE

Dee Dee Kiesow

I remembered saying goodbye to my brother, when I was in kindergarten, as he left for Vietnam. The year was 1967. He was my best friend, and he sent me letters I still read and treasure to this day. After he completed his tour of duty, my brother returned home an empty shell of his former self and an addict. I was in third grade when he returned, and I loved President Nixon for bringing him home with scars and all.

Fast forward to 2024, and I am with a special veteran's project group visiting the bunker *below the* Tomb of the Unknown Soldier, a place I had only heard of and never visited. We descended the cement steps slowly and solemnly, not fully knowing what to expect. It is hallowed ground, unknown to most, and yet it remains one of the most sacred places in the United States. I was overcome emotionally and kept silently chiding myself to 'hold it together' while trying to appear dignified... and not release the tears that threatened to spill.

The bunker is located beyond a sea of more than 400,000 white granite tombstones and beneath the Tomb of the Unknown Soldier at Arlington National Cemetery. Here, elite soldiers of the 3rd U.S. Infantry Regiment ("The Old Guard") clean weapons and prepare for the Changing of the Guard Ceremony. Before exiting the bunker, we paid homage to one of our own, a guard on their history wall (gunned down in Afghanistan), and caught glimpses of the tiny kitchen, meeting rooms, walls covered with uniform pieces, American flags, memorabilia, awards, and security cameras. Before our exit, we handled several weapons used over the years by the esteemed guard, both living and dead.

Above the bunker, members of a family placed a wreath during the traditional ceremony for their loved one. My heart sank for them, especially the mother. Her outer strength and loving heart placed others ahead of herself, despite her grief, which she kept hidden behind a steely smile. Earlier, she had called me out of my entourage and given me a hug. I felt unworthy.

Soon, we would gather in a light rain to board a bus and visit yet another tombstone placed atop another fallen hero. I do not know the circumstances of that hero, but I am keenly aware that many will mourn for decades because of them. I find comfort in the words of my friend: Major General Kent Hillhouse, U.S. Army (retired) Vietnam War Veteran, Purple Heart Recipient with Oak Leaf Cluster.

"I made sure my guys knew that my goal was to ensure their safe return home. Obviously, that did not always happen. But at least they knew I was not making irrational decisions and I was trying to keep them alive."

We have come to trust the decisions of our leaders in spite of a zero-sum victory in our most recent wars. It's always someone else's call, someone else's watch. I was called to serve those who served, and in retrospect, I can see that I sacrificed a piece of me in the process. I cried, I mourned, and as an empath, I felt every bit of trauma and pain I encountered as if it were my own. I learned that from my own years of abuse in foster care; I can read it in the eyes of others and feel it like a gong in my soul when I enter a room.

Our next stop was the gymnasium. We were told to queue in the stands . . . and then it happened. In full regalia, out came the United

States Army Old Guard Fife and Drum Corps. Their tradition dates back to the birth of our nation, and we were primed for a private concert. I teared up for most of the concert, then we were invited down to meet the musical Guards. After a while, our host asked for silence, then he called out my name. I was frozen in disbelief. I had a hand in creating the event as a part of our campaign, but it was nothing I would consider remarkable. I was gifted a beautiful shadowbox bearing a horseshoe. Then the following words were read: "This horseshoe was used during a Military Full Honors Funeral in Arlington National Cemetery. Dedicated to Dee Dee Kiesow by the 3rd US Infantry Regiment, The Old Guard."

Eighteen months earlier, I enthusiastically answered a call of duty to realize a bigger-than-life vision that would eventually include powerful and influential people. The journey would require me to travel coast to coast and would involve hopscotching visits to humble homes across the heartland . . . and would conclude at the White House.

The mission was to save the lives of soldiers who served in the Afghanistan war. It is a little-known fact that twenty-two veterans die each day by suicide. *Each day.* In one of the wealthiest countries in the world. I instinctively wanted to save the lives of soldiers and veterans, who, like my brother, could not get the help they needed when they needed it. Little did I know that in the process of completing our mission, one of the lives I saved would be my own.

In 2020, much like everyone, COVID had put the brakes on my nonprofit consulting business, and I was looking for something bigger with purpose that I could contribute to. I was meeting with a community leader to whom I had been introduced, and I suddenly had a vision of the most successful organization ever. As a nonprofit executive, I'm wired for optimism . . . and I immediately saw victory in donors, doers, collaborators, community . . . and most of all the veterans to whom this community leader's organization could deliver new hope. It seems funny to say now, but the concept of establishing a foundation to help combat veterans find hope and connect to their community again first appeared on a cocktail napkin in a hotel bar in Las Vegas.

And then reality settled in. I soon discovered raising money for veterans suffering from the invisible disease of Post Traumatic Stress Disorder (PTSD) would not be easy. After calling one hundred veteran-oriented support organizations and individuals for our first campaign, I got ninety-six "no's and ghosts."

Combat-related PTSD is invisible, yet it is a living monster if you've got it in your head. It comes with a stare so cold at times that it could pierce your heart. It brings flashbacks, depression, the inability to focus on completing a task, the inability to "fit in" upon return home, and, most difficult of all, to be the person you once were, for friends and loved ones. I know because my brother was divorced several times, leaving his sons behind because his wife was "too controlling." Having observed my brother's quiet trauma, my family knew better, and it still tore us apart.

Back on the campaign trail, in less than two months, we raised enough money to bring veterans together for meet-ups and courses on Zoom initially, and then later, in person.

On one campaign stop, I found myself in the woods with two dozen combat veterans. I hadn't been adventuring and hiking like that before, and I instantly recognized it was as special for them as it was for me. Can I just tell you? Soldiers really know how to build amazing campfires! The fire was big and warm, and the flames danced for hours as stories were shared around the blazing embers. Someone made me toasted marshmallows on a big stick, a special treat. I was given access to the 'inner circle' and I found that 'little sister' feeling I had known long ago.

But that primal feeling of a little girl's trust soon opened a wound in my heart that bled directly into my soul. I tried to ignore it. I was sitting among giants, among heroes telling stories about their darkly lived experience, trying to make sense of an insensible situation while they bravely carried out duties they were trained to perform. By turns, the conversation would swerve toward body bags, someone's pet being shot in the head, death, injustice, burn pits, cancer, racism, death, more death, and suicide. It was all too much, and I began having trouble sleeping all night. I didn't know what to do but cry. So, I did.

What I didn't expect was the campaign to thrust me from my comfort zone on a daily basis, to creating new levels of integrity within myself. I expected no less from others, but when my expectations were not met, my deeper wounds of abuse and betrayal were triggered, and I had to face my own monster. Add some PTSD to the recipe, and several stressors too many, and I had the winning recipe for a disaster.

I am not ashamed to say that all the darkness I thought I was working to alleviate finally came to land. An interpersonal conflict developed during the campaign wherein I was the subject of vitriol, and it became increasingly clear that I had to either concede or walk away. I had a secret stash of pills at home in case that day ever came, and at one point, I thought it had. Then, a combat veteran, a trained killer, the recipient of valor with lots of colorful medals, made me pinky promise I wouldn't die by suicide, *ever*. He promised the same to me, and we linked our pinkies like nine-year-old BFFs making a pinkie promise. We looked into each other's eyes and nodded. I felt safe for a while.

While the veterans project was thriving, I found myself sinking into depression. I loved the project so much that I tried to push through, to 'soldier on' and appease or deflect the source of ill-treatment, but I wasn't always successful. One day, as I was doing the work that was so vital to the success of the project, I was on the receiving end of a vicious tirade.

I began shaking like a leaf, and a soldier turned to me and said, "Dee Dee, I'm sorry you're dragging your butt in the dirt today. I know it's my fault because you manage to absorb it all."

I was stunned and very embarrassed. Later, we were in public, and the soldier turned and asked me what he should do next. I knew just what to say. "Stop dragging your butt in the dirt, Soldier, and smile and be kind to all the people." He laughed, took a selfie, and did just that. I was relieved.

Before my final trip to DC, I got the courage to find my brother. I hadn't seen him since he disappeared somewhere in the 1980s. I knocked on the door of his tiny one-room apartment to no avail and proceeded to wait in my car for hours. The next day, I knocked on a neighbor's door. When there was still no answer at my brother's place, she called his cell phone. A woman answered, identifying herself as a nurse at a local hospital where my brother had been brought in after suffering a stroke. She held the phone to his ear, and I told him I loved him. It was the last time we spoke.

I'm self-aware enough to know that not every situation is meant to last a lifetime, so when given the chance, we must follow our heart and look for the good. I know a bunch of brave guys who are alive right now and well because they are finding their purpose beyond killing, beyond survival, beyond despair. They belong to one another again and find well-being because someone cared enough to try to make a difference, to offer respite. If given the chance, these emotionally wounded veterans want to connect with people who know and understand them.

There is a virtuous cycle of feeling good and doing good. My 'dark night' experience didn't actually kill me; it made me stronger than ever before. It required everything I had to uplevel, focus on the mission, and set in motion a new way of living and supporting veterans. We accomplished what had never been done before. I had never been challenged mentally, physically, or professionally so dramatically, and I am grateful to have those effects ripple into the world. It's true that what doesn't break us does make us more resilient.

I've discovered that sometimes the ripple effect only shows up when you reach the end of everything you know. Sometimes the end of what you know isn't the end at all, but an invitation to expand. It isn't always easy, but it works, I promise.

Make that a pinky promise.

"On one campaign stop, I found myself in the woods with two dozen combat veterans. I hadn't been adventuring and hiking like that before, and I instantly recognized it was as special for them as it was for me."

4
DOG + PONY SHOW

Catherine Kaufer

Everyone has a COVID story, and this is one of them, but my story began years before. It just so happens that on May 5, 2015, Cinco de Mayo, I received a text from my husband, George. I had just completed a presentation to a new buyer at my office and was on my way home when I noticed a text from him. I vividly recall the timestamp, which said 4:52.

'Hey! I got off early, went to the dentist, and now I'm going out for a bike ride. Will you pick me up from Mark's at 7:30?'

This wasn't unusual, as George loved to ride, so I replied, *'Sure'* and went on with gearing down from the day, getting ready to go pick up some takeout.

A bit later, I'm puttering around, whittling away time until I have to pick him up. Then, at 6:05, my phone rang. I didn't recognize the number, but since it was local and I'm a realtor, I decided to pick up the call.

The voice on the other end asked, "Is this Catherine Kaufer?"

"Yes," I replied, "It is."

The caller identified herself, and I don't really remember her name, but when she said John Muir Hospital, a chill zipped up my spine.

She said, "Your husband is George Kaufer, correct?"

"Yes," I whispered.

"There's been an accident," the woman said. "We had to Life Flight him here. Right now he's stable, but you need to come to the hospital as soon as you can."

I said nothing, and she continued.

"Please have someone pick you up and drive you because we don't want you to get in an accident getting here because you're upset."

When we hung up, I called my girlfriend, Vicki. When she answered, I blurted, "Vicki, can you pick me up? George has been in an accident, and I need to get to John Muir."

"Of course!" she agreed.

I waited for what seemed like forever and began to fill the time by notifying friends and family, especially our two daughters. "George has been in an accident," I said. I told them to go to John Muir and pray like they've never prayed before.

At 5:30, Vicki called back. "I can't get to you," she said. "The roads are closed. Something happened, and there are emergency vehicles everywhere."

We didn't know then that George *was* the accident. Paramedics, police, and firefighters had responded and were jamming up the roads.

"Cath," Vicki said. "I can't get to you. You have to try to go yourself."

When I arrive at the hospital, the waiting room is filled with George's friends and family. I'm both numb and overwhelmed by the outpouring of love. I learn then that two of his best friends have already called our church pastor to come.

I am only there a few minutes when a police officer arrives. I am asked for the second time that afternoon, "Are you Catherine Kaufer?"

I reply, "I am."

"We need to speak right away," the officer says.

My gaze locks onto my brother, and he joins me. When we walk into the small room that she leads us to, she sits behind a desk and says to me, "Will you sit down?"

I say, "No. I can't. Just tell me."

I watch too much TV not to know that nothing good comes when they tell you to sit down. "I can't do it," I murmur, and start crying, and she says, *"Please. I need you to sit down."* So, I sit.

"Your husband was on his bike, and a woman ran the red light."

With cold dread, I learned my beautiful George ricocheted off her windshield and was thrown one hundred feet. His bicycle was thrown two hundred feet, with parts scattered all over the road.

"He's fighting for his life right now, and he's on life support. I need you to talk to the doctor first, and then you can see him."

I nod and cling to my brother's hand.

"They are trying to keep him alive . . . but he's fighting it."

When I speak with the physician in charge, he reports that George is brain dead and was probably dead at impact.

I stand there, bathed in the surreal light of a hospital ER bay, in a chorus of machines and personnel, trying to absorb what is happening.

One doctor with a kind face asks me in measured tones, "Was your husband an athlete?"

Stunned and weeping, I said, "Yes. He is. And riding his bike is his peace. It's, you know, his chill time and . . ."

My voice falters. I don't admit that I always feared this was the way he would die. Every time he'd go out to ride his bike, I would silently pray for him. But for some reason that day, I did not. I just didn't. Thoughts crowd my mind, and even in this chaos, in a matter-of-fact way, I know that George died loving what he was doing, and as a man of faith, he didn't fear death or what comes after. They take us to George's bed, and we are given thirty minutes to say our goodbyes.

He is on life support, surrounded by medical equipment under harsh fluorescent lights. I can see the EKG, recording a heartbeat that his brain betrays. It is weird, seeing his face, and even though he has no bruises, he is very battered. My body quivers with shock, and I turn to the kind doctor.

"You need to tell us what to . . . you need to tell us what to do next. I already know he doesn't want to be on life support. He's not afraid."

I scan the curtained 'room' where George lies still and silent. "Can we invite his friends in? Can everyone come up with me?"

The medical team agrees, so I lead an entourage to George's bed, and we form a circle around him. I hold his hand. Our dearest friends and family begin saying goodbye to this good man, and the medics hover nearby, sponging away the blood that keeps leaking out of him and cannot be stopped.

An older, experienced nurse approached me and whispers, "He can hear you. You need to talk to him."

So I keep talking to George, even though his hand is very cold. I know even as the medical teams keep his heart beating artificially, my George, my husband, my girls' Dad, is no longer here.

I watch his vitals begin to fail on the monitor like a clock winding down. Finally, I straighten my shoulder and take a quivering breath. "Okay," I say. "It's time."

The pastors come in and they pray for me, for everybody, for George. And then it's over, and it is peaceful.

A physician steps forward and says, "Your daughters are on their way. Go to them, take them home, and tell them. Don't let them see their Dad this way. You don't want them to remember him like this."

When we arrive at the house sometime later, they follow me in asking, "How's Dad?" I make it to the top step of the stairs. I remember the moment with crystal clarity, knowing that what I say will change everything for them.

"Come here," I say. "I have something I need to tell you."

But they aren't having it. "No, no, no," they chorus.

"Dad's gone. I'm sorry," I say, as if I could change it.

"But you told me he was just . . ." Janelle says.

And I think to myself: *I came to the hospital expecting a long recovery. I wasn't expecting him to be dead. They didn't tell me that on the phone.*

"They told me not to tell you."

Megan wants to see him, wants "proof" this wasn't a horrible hoax. Janelle accepts the fact and doesn't need the details.

"I'm sorry," I say to my girls. "He's gone." I don't tell them that night that the girl whose car hit him was their age. She was just trying to change the radio station and drove through a red light into the intersection as George was crossing it.

Looking back, I see them in the foyer of the house they grew up in, at the bottom of the stairs, broken from the truth of it all. And then I remember that two weeks before the accident, George came home from a trip to Colorado, after spending time with his dad and his brother in a kind of mini-reunion.

When he came home, we were at the dinner table talking about his trip. He said, "Cath, I have this weird feeling."

He told me about the great time with his brother and his dad, and then he said, "I just have this really weird feeling that's not going away."

Naturally concerned, I said, "What is it?"

For a minute, looking like the young man I married 29 years before, he says, "I'm going to be fifty-six in June, and I can't imagine myself being older than fifty-five. So, if something's . . . if something happens to me and I'm in an accident and I'm on life support, I know where I'm going. Take me off."

He went on to tell me what he wanted for his memorial. But we had talked about our legacy plans before, so I already knew all that. So I went, *'yeah, yeah, you'll be fine.'* In that moment, I didn't remember. I didn't remember until later that God had forewarned me that George's life would be cut short.

In 2005, I had a premonition that there would be a tragedy in my family. God told me my grandpa was going to die. He also told me when my grandma was going to die. He also told me that in the next five years, I would experience a tragedy in my family.

In the meantime, George worked through a bad business deal that brought him to his knees and shook him up so much that he changed his life and the way he was operating. But the bad business deal actually shook him to the foundation and transformed him. It was like God took him down to the core and rebuilt him up.

After that, George was a changed man, a man of faith, the husband I always wanted. And I think that's why, in 2015, he told me. *'I know where I'm going,'* because he did.

I talk to God frequently; it's the relationship I have with Him. God had told me when I was pregnant with my youngest, in 1993, that my grandpa would not see *her,* but at that time, *I didn't know if* it was a girl or a boy. So I was at my grandpa's funeral, and I was pregnant with her. He also said that Monique, who was Grandpa's wife at the time, would pass two years after, and she did, almost to the day.

Back in 2014, a year before George died, I received my Ministry license. I always knew that I wanted to do something with a miniature horse and a miniature Australian shepherd, some type of pet therapy to help people heal. But I didn't know what, because usually the miniature horses are typically reserved for autistic kids or people with disabilities, right? Well, it's not what God had in mind for me at all. But I didn't know that. I used to ride bikes with George, and we were in Solvang, and I fell and broke my elbow.

So there I am, a one-armed bandit, and unable to do much out at the ranch where I kept my horse. I called one of my girlfriends, and I said, "Hey, Lisa, do you know anyone who could help me with my horse?" Since I had a broken elbow and I couldn't shovel stuff out of Jag's stall, I really need someone. "I need someone to help."

Lisa replied, "You need to call Christina."

So, I called Christina, met her, and we got along great. She loved my horse. Not too long after that, Christina's mom came to where I kept my horse and said, "Cath, I heard you got your ministry license. What do you want to do with it?"

I had been thinking about this and quickly said, "I've always wanted a miniature horse to do pet therapy with."

Her eyes sparkled, and she said, "I know a miniature horse farm. Let me see if they have a horse they can give you."

Two weeks later, on Good Friday, I took delivery of a little one-year-old mini that came in an extra-large dog crate. Good Friday, right? And then George met him, and he said, "I think God is setting you up for a ministry."

"Do you think so?" I replied.

"I do," George said, grinning the way he always did.

And that's how Zeby came to be my therapy horse. Two weeks after George died, I was gifted a mini–Australian Shepherd. It was like my two therapy animals were hand-picked by God. And when people heard my story, they wanted to help. Zeby was free. A miniature horse, just a baby. No papers, no nothing, valued at $2,500.

Zeby became my first therapy animal, and then, two weeks after George died, I was gifted a miniature Australian shepherd.

Horses as a whole have a bigger energy field than we do, which is one of the reasons why they are such great therapy animals. So they're called majestic because their heartbeat is so much lower than ours, and when we're around them, our heartbeat matches their heartbeat, and they calm us down. And Zeby's so easy, he'll just put his head in the lap of someone in a wheelchair. He's two feet tall, so he just puts his head on their lap. And they see his little face, and they light up.

Before George died, I was just a wife and a mother and a realtor. Now, as an ordained minister, I bring a smile to people's faces and make them happy. I went through life coaching classes and took all the steps, not knowing exactly where it would lead. Like in *Field of Dreams*, I just kept '*building it.*' It wasn't till George died that I knew I would be helping women through trauma and loss. Now, I'm certified in Equine Therapy. The whole time, God had his eye on this sparrow and gave me what I needed for the next step in the journey. Now it's God and me and my dog and pony show.

5
BECAUSE PETS ARE FAMILY

Anna M. van Heeckeren, DVM, MS

I've loved animals forever—one of my earliest memories as a little girl is sitting in a whelping pen, enjoying the pile of black and yellow Labrador puppies that climbed all over me. It was pure joy. I "inherited" this passion from my mom, who collected many types of animals. They were an integral part of my life growing up, and I actively took part in their care. Those early experiences taught me the joys, challenges, and responsibilities of living with and caring for animals.

Alongside my mom's influence, my dad also shaped my career path in a different but equally important way. He was a cardiothoracic surgeon, and his dedication to medicine inspired my own commitment to healing. I chose to focus on helping animals, much to my father's chagrin. He thought I'd be good at human medicine when I helped him put his shoulder back in place after he dislocated it during a sailboat race. With a love of animals and a commitment to helping them through medical care, I was driven to become a veterinarian.

I got great advice about making me a strong candidate to get accepted into veterinary school: get a variety of different experiences working in veterinary medicine, get good grades, and expect rejection the first time you apply.

I volunteered for different kinds of veterinary practitioners who helped dogs, cats, horses, and cattle. I worked in a heavy metal toxicology lab for two summers in research related to aquatic animal medicine.

I took the same classes pre-med students take, earning a bachelor's degree in biology. I have to admit, undergraduate school was hard. My grades were OK, but I had a "D" on my report card—I wasn't surprised when I was rejected that first year. To improve my chances, I earned a master's degree in molecular genetics with great grades, and that did the trick. I was accepted to The Ohio State University College of Veterinary Medicine. Woohoo!

I found veterinary school challenging. So much to memorize! But I did well and passed the veterinary board exams. After considering several types of opportunities, I decided to take a job offer at a dog and cat hospital in Detroit, MI. My career path was taking shape.

But life took an unexpected turn before graduation. In February, a classmate and I were traveling to spend time with a practicing veterinarian a few hours away from campus. Only miles away from our destination, we were in a near-fatal car accident.

Fortunately, I was allowed to graduate in 1993 and make up for the classwork I missed while in the hospital (seventeen days!). I went back home to finish my recovery with occupational therapy and learned that the job I secured was no longer available because of the duration of my recovery time and their policy about accepting new graduates.

This unexpected change in my career path forced me to ask: *Now what?* Always looking for the silver lining, I realized my options were expansive. The world was my oyster, given my education and experiences. It was exciting and a little scary.

In my career search, I met my now husband, and I was drawn to cystic fibrosis research—not because of a personal connection, but because I found it a fascinating disease to study. It brought together my knowledge of comparative anatomy, biology, medicine, and genetics, and I wanted to help find a cure for people suffering from this horrible, inherited disease.

During my 15 years at Case Western Reserve University (CWRU), my husband introduced me to the importance of philanthropy. He encouraged me to support causes close to my heart. For me, that meant supporting veterinary-related organizations focused on animal health and welfare, including the American Veterinary Medical Foundation (AVMF).

Given my loyal support, the AVMF Executive Director wanted to know more about me. When they learned about my research experience, I was asked to serve on a Committee in 2002 and invited to serve on the Board of Directors in 2003. Serving on the AVMF Board was a passion of mine for many years.

While working at CWRU and thinking about my passion for animal welfare, I would sit and wonder: *Is this [my job] why I became a veterinarian?* For many years, the answer was, *"No, but the job is rewarding in many ways and I feel like I'm making a difference."*

The next pivotal moment in my career path was in 2005. I attended an American Veterinary Medical Association (AVMA) conference where President Dr. Roger Mahr spoke about the concept of *One Health*—the fact that human, animal, and environmental health are deeply interconnected.

Wow! *One Health* was a concept that inspired me to consider: *How do we bring this big, global idea down to the local level? How do we make it relevant to people's everyday lives?*

As the economy faltered, I learned that when people's budgets got really tight, they weren't taking their pets to the veterinarian. That's not just an animal welfare issue—it's a public health concern.

So in 2008, inspired by *One Health* and drawing on my experiences at CWRU and AVMF, I founded a nonprofit organization with the purpose of creating equitable, affordable, sustainable healthcare systems to benefit the health of people and animals in their shared environments.

The first name of the nonprofit was *The van Bakeren Foundation*—a playful blend of my last name, van Heeckeren, and my husband's last name, Baker. An aunt had affectionately nicknamed us *The van Bakerens*, and my husband and I loved it. Not all family members loved it, and it made us sound like a family foundation giving out money to other nonprofits, so we kept rethinking the name choice.

I was initially a little shy about using *"One Health"* in the name, knowing the important work happening at the national and international levels. However, one of our contract employees identified a human health care group in California that owned the domain name OneHealth.org. They were not using it, and we were able to purchase it at a reasonable price in 2010.

Over time, we realized that other groups forming around the *One Health* concept were choosing longer names, and we owned a perfectly simple domain name. So we said, *Why not rename our nonprofit 'One Health Organization'?* It just made sense, so we rebranded in 2012.

Access to veterinary care is crucial for people living with or near animals. As stated in the Veterinarian's Oath, we are public health professionals because we prevent the accidental spread of diseases from animals to people (aka zoonotic diseases).

Years ago, many people interacted with animals kept as livestock and protected them from the dangers of exposure to wildlife. Veterinary care initially focused on keeping these animals healthy. While this is still a high priority, government agencies involved in public health across the globe also focus on the most dangerous zoonotic diseases.

Today, most people's exposure to animals is their pets—mostly dogs and cats. They are companions and considered part of the family. Many people even call themselves pet parents. Some bristle at that idea because "animals aren't children," but for most, pets *are* family. Research conducted through the Human-Animal Bond Research Institute (HABRI) shows that the emotional bond we have with our pets benefits us physically, emotionally, and psychologically.

The importance of access to veterinary care was highlighted for me when I served on the AVMF Board in 2005 during Hurricane Katrina. Pets were part of that disaster, or *were* the disaster. Recovery efforts were more difficult for first responders who weren't allowed to rescue pets or other animals—only people. Many shelter pets and people's pets lacked veterinary care before the disaster, so the diseases they carried were spread in areas that weren't heavily impacted before.

The importance of helping people pay for veterinary care was highlighted for me when I served on several public health committees. Most non-veterinary public health providers had no appreciation that the cost of vaccines and parasite control, which prevent many common zoonotic diseases, must be paid by the pet owners, and that an estimated 50 percent of pet owners weren't providing any veterinary care.

There are many beliefs about pets and their people. Some people believe that…

Pets are a luxury. But anyone can have a pet, and poverty is a reality for far too many. Pets enrich our lives—they make life worth living, they bring us joy, and they don't care how much money their people have. I'd rather see a pet in a loving home than in a shelter.

Low-income people don't care about their pets. We know that they care enough about their pets to seek veterinary care and pay for it. They know they have a responsibility to their pets. Often, they will sacrifice what little money they have to care for their pets rather than take care of themselves. It hurts pets if their people don't take care of themselves first.

Pet care should be free for anyone who can't afford it. Just like physicians in human healthcare, veterinarians need to be paid for their work. Veterinary staff love animals and need to earn a living. Anyone who has taken their pet to a veterinary clinic knows the bills can be overwhelming. Many people can get help affording veterinary care by getting pet insurance or getting a small loan through CareCredit. Unfortunately, pet insurance does not start with wellness care, and not everyone qualifies for CareCredit.

If their pet doesn't look sick, they don't need veterinary care. At a minimum, each pet needs annual wellness care, which means a physical exam once a year and addressing any other needs, such as vaccinations, parasite control, and routine tests. It all adds up. And if extra tests, like radiographs (X-rays) and ultrasounds, prescription diets, or surgery are needed, the cost goes up even higher.

Ever since its inception, I wanted to fill an unmet need that used my education, experiences, and skills. We believe that no person or pet should suffer from a lack of access to veterinary care. That conviction drives everything we do.

Initially, One Health Organization focused on supporting older adults living with dogs and cats and covering wellness care—older adults often live on a fixed and limited income, and the cost of veterinary care can be too expensive. We believed they may also lack transportation, so we created a program called *Vets On Wheels* that brought veterinary care directly to seniors in pet-friendly residential facilities. While meaningful and convenient, it wasn't sustainable.

Today, our signature *Veterinary Care Voucher Card Program* provides financial assistance to help people afford veterinary care for their dogs and cats.

One Health Organization serves households at or below 200 percent of the federal poverty level—about $30,000 a year, or roughly $2,500 a month, for a single person. We offer up to $250 on a Veterinary Care Voucher Card per household per year, which helps cover the cost of basic veterinary care for one healthy pet. The total value we provide to pet parents costs $1,500 per household.

As of this writing, we've supported over 2,000 veterinary visits for dogs and over 1,000 for cats. We've partnered with 66 veterinary clinics over the years that accept our Voucher Cards as payment. Together, we've helped provide nearly $430,000 in veterinary care to families and their pets.

Helping people access veterinary care is at the core of what we do. As the visionary for One Health Organization, I have way too many ideas for programs beyond the Voucher Program. What I know is that healthy and happy pets need their people to be healthy and happy, too. So our strategic direction is to focus my creative energy on streamlining and expanding the Voucher Program outside of Northeast Ohio and partnering with other organizations that can help the people we serve access social services.

While many people understandably focus on making sure humans or homeless pets are fed, housed, and cared for, what makes One Health Organization different is that we work to *increase access to "veterinary" care*. I put "veterinary" in quotation marks because we recognize that caring for animals in a household means caring for the people who care for them.

In our own way, I like to think that our mission helps increase happiness and healthfulness—and that makes this second-generation pet lover's heart happy.

"Pets enrich our lives—they make life worth living, they bring us joy, and they don't care how much money their people have. I'd rather see a pet in a loving home than in a shelter."

6

THE DESK MOMENT:
Redefining Success on My Own Terms

Sarah Olivieri, MPS

They say life can change in a moment. I don't know if that's true for everyone, but I know the exact moment my life pivoted.

I was sitting at a tiny desk tucked into the unfinished attic of a boyfriend's house where I was staying…temporarily…in the middle of a divorce, broke (I had $35 in my bank account), and a single mom to a three-year-old. I had just come home from a divorce mediation session with a blank custody calendar in hand. My job: decide how to split parenting time with my son's father.

That same day, I'd been in a mastermind session about scaling a service business. The topic? The value of your time. Specifically, how owning your time is the key to owning your future. It was the first time anyone had laid it out so plainly: if you want to scale, you can't do everything yourself—your hours are limited. My assignment: figure out the key activities that were worth $1000/hour and eliminate or delegate everything else.

So, I sat at that tiny desk with a pen in hand. I knew I wanted to prioritize my time with my son. At the time, I would have called that an instinctual imperative. Today, I would call it values-driven decision making, choosing to spend my energy and resources on the activities that I most enjoy; those activities that are enjoyable even when they are hard. And at that desk, I realized that leaving my husband and changing my business were all tied to a new understanding of how valuable and precious time is. Time, not money, is the resource that gives us access to quality relationships, community, knowledge, and wisdom. In other words, it's time, not money, that brings us joy and fulfillment. Unfortunately, too often we are surrounded by the pervasive lie that money brings happiness.

From that day on, I have lived by a powerful quote: *"You can make up for lost money, but you can't make up for lost time."*

So with time for things that matter to me as the priority, I pulled out my calculator and did the math. (Pro tip: always run the numbers.) I looked at the calendar. I totaled up how many hours per week I could work if I prioritized time with my son. The numbers on that page are permanently burned in my mind: 28.5 one week and 31 hours the next. That was all I had to build my business, earn a livable income, and keep us afloat.

Then I did the rest of the math: my monthly expenses, savings goals, modest dreams for our lifestyle, and a retirement fund I hadn't even started. What I came up with was this:

I needed to earn $120,000 per year.

I could only work 28.5 hours a week.

And the work had to feel meaningful.

That moment changed everything. That was the moment I put a stake in the ground and pivoted towards joy and fulfillment.

This wouldn't be the last time I carefully evaluated my time. Today, it's a daily habit to evaluate how much time it's worth investing in any activity. When I'm working, I track my time and then evaluate where it's going every two months.

If I am leaving a legacy of impact in the wake of my life, it's probably spreading the word about valuing time and enjoying how you spend it.

Most recently, I had the great privilege and joy of trailering my J/80 sailboat to Annapolis to skipper my first level race (that's racing against the same kind of boat) at the 2025 Helly Hansen Sailing World Regatta. Unfortunately, as I prepared my boat for the race, I discovered an issue with the bottom paint flaking off in places. I repaired it, and then more problem areas emerged. It was so aggravating . . . and in case you haven't found yourself working on bottom paint issues, I can tell you that it sucks! You are working with toxic substances over your head while half crouched down. And then there is lots of sanding and burnishing. At first, it was fun, because a perfectly smooth bottom makes your boat fast, but when the second round of paint chips emerged, still with a long pre-departure to-do list, I re-evaluated and decided the gain was not worth the pain. I had higher-value things to attend to. This first regatta for me was about getting there, doing the regatta, and having fun. A few paint chips wouldn't get in the way of that. In the end, it was the right call. I achieved all these things, plus three surprise wins, but not without some bumps in the road.

On the evening of the second of three days of racing, I found myself down two crew members. My remaining crew members were very worried. I was not. Time gives you access to quality relationships with smart and generous people, and I'd built some good ones in the sailing community. I reached out to everyone I knew, and through a friend of a friend, I found a replacement crew who was an incredible racer. Bonus win #1: I made a fantastic new sailing friend.

Thanks to having a crew familiar with the boat and level racing, on day three, I took sixth out of 22 very competitive boats in one race. I'm still glowing with gratitude and pride for that win.

And for the third bonus win, my joyful energy attracted the attention of the editor of *Sailing World* magazine, who wrote a feature article about me, my sailing journey, my bottom paint, and my commitment to having a good time, spreading my message to an additional 20,000+ people.

Before that attic-desk moment, I'd already left a successful run as an executive director. On paper, I was good at the job. Our programs were working, we were growing, and our board was happy. But I never felt successful—not in a way that mattered.

I raised money, I designed and launched programs, I engaged with stakeholders, but I was chasing goals that weren't mine. Running on "shoulds" and achieving the dreams of other people.

That's the trap so many leaders fall into: we define success by external standards. Growth. Revenue. Recognition. We check boxes but feel empty. And the nonprofit world isn't exactly designed to make it easy to thrive. We're taught to sacrifice, to always give more, to hustle harder. Burnout is worn like a badge.

I had seen my own mother do this. She had saved the small, independent school I had attended from going under financially. I used to say she opened up her veins and bled for that school. I still think of her working in the summer upstairs in a very hot, small office. No one else worked in the summer, but there she was plugging away, putting all the pieces into place ... sweating. She finally splurged one year and got a tiny window AC for her office. That's just how it is for so many nonprofit leaders.

But deep down, I knew there had to be a better way. As I made my way, I learned three crucial lessons for achieving success on my own terms.

Lesson 1: Stay in the Game

One thing I had going for me, even in the chaos, was my

persistence. I kept showing up. I kept iterating. I kept tweaking what wasn't working and doubling down on what was.

Looking back, I realize this was my first big lesson learned in success: staying in the game. That sounds almost too simple, but it's powerful. I wasn't "failing fast"—I was learning slowly but surely. Each attempt brought new insights. I saw patterns. I built resilience. I was determined to find a better way, to make my own better way.

Most people quit too soon. They think if it doesn't work right away, they're doing it wrong. But honestly, I think half the battle is just *not quitting*, not giving up. You have to hold on to the belief that everything is figure-outable and stay in the game.

And yes, it was messy. There were ups and downs. The journey isn't linear, and still the wins add up, and each setback is just one more rabbit hole to avoid, even if you have to run down it three more times before you finally stop going in there.

Lesson 2: Get Specific About What Success Looks Like

That second lesson hit me like lightning at the attic desk: I had never actually defined what success looked like for me. Not in a concrete, add-it-up-with-a-calculator kind of way. We throw the word around constantly—success. But what does it really mean?

For me, in that moment, it meant being *time-rich*. It meant doing work that filled my soul, while being fully present for the little boy who needed me most. It meant spending my time pursuing what I wanted, rather than checking off boxes for someone else.

That was the gift of the parenting calendar: it forced me to face my reality and take ownership of my time. I didn't want to squeeze in bedtime stories between email replies. I didn't want to feel guilty every time I closed my laptop. And I sure as heck didn't want to build a business that just became another cage.

So, I committed to building a business that fit *my life*, not the other way around.

Lesson 3: Stick to the Plan

A few months later, I stumbled onto the third key to success: intention. Or, as I started calling it, "sticking to the plan."

Once you know what you want, it's amazing how many shiny objects try to distract you. New ideas. Bigger opportunities. Pressure from clients. Social media. Your own inner voice telling you to do more, be more, push harder.

But success isn't just about knowing your plan. It's about *honoring* it.

That meant saying no. A lot. No to the extra projects. No to networking events that don't align. No to reactivity. I had a goal: $120K/year, 28.5 hours a week, meaningful work. If a decision didn't get me closer to that, it was a no.

That discipline changed my business—and my life—and ultimately became a system that I now have the joy of teaching others.

I didn't invent my system overnight. It started with borrowing and cobbling. I pulled ideas from everywhere: Agile, EOS, *The Great Game of Business*, OKRs, even systems thinking and communication frameworks from folks like Margaret Wheatley and Marshall Rosenberg.

Some pieces clicked. Some didn't. But my inner strategist loved the challenge. It was getting easier to stay in the game, and the big goals were now broken into clear, specific sub-goals, and sticking to the plan was getting easier and easier.

Soon, my business was humming. And then something amazing happened: my clients started noticing. They wanted to know how I was getting so much done in so few hours. They wanted to know how I stayed clearheaded. They wanted the system.

At first, though, I couldn't give it to them without them learning everything I had learned. It was a set of tools and processes, but not a repeatable system. Something still wasn't right. There was nothing to glue it all together. I had pulled from so many sources and made so many modifications, it was messy! There had to be a better way; a streamlined, simple, easy-to-use, easy to learn method.

"There has to be a better way" echoes over and over in my head whenever I'm in problem-solving mode, and one night it just wouldn't leave me be. I found myself late at night at my dining room table with papers outlining the parts of the system everywhere. I was shuffling them around, and I filled in the gaps. I stripped away the extra layers. And I wove in the missing pieces: capacity building, mission alignment, and the human side of nonprofit work. I kept adding pages and removing pages until finally it clicked . . . and I had a "Eureka" moment. I figured out how to tie everything together, and the Impact Method® was born.

The results? More impact. More clarity. Less burnout. And for me? More time. I now work just 16 hours a week—three focused, purposeful days—and I still generate results that make me proud. Not just in my business, but for my clients, my family, and myself.

Here's the part I want you to hear loud and clear: your version of success gets to be yours. It doesn't have to match anyone else's. It doesn't have to be about more, bigger, faster.

It can be about *enough*. It can be about peace. It can be about being time-rich, results-rich, joy-rich.

If you're leading a nonprofit—or any mission-driven work—you already care deeply. That's a strength. But without a clear definition of success, you'll burn out chasing other people's goals.

So take a moment. Grab a pen and a calculator. Ask yourself:

~ How much time do I really want to spend working?

~ What do I want my life to feel like?

~ What would success look like if no one else were watching?

Then, get specific. Do the math. Map it out. And stick to the plan.

That day in the attic wasn't magical. It was practical. But sometimes practicality is the most loving thing we can offer ourselves.

I didn't wait for someone to give me permission to define success. I claimed it. I built it. I lived into it.

And today, I have a life I love. I work 16 hours a week. I help nonprofits thrive. I go sailing with my dad, fishing with my son, and I'm planning my next chapter of adventures in marriage . . . I have the energy and the time to be present for what I value. That's my success.

It's not flashy. But it's mine. And it's enough.

7
THE BEST DAY OF MY LIFE

Brandon Peacock

They say your life can change in a moment. Mine did—with the crack of a 9mm pistol.

It was 5:45 pm after a long workday. I was twenty-three, heading to the barber shop for my typical monthly haircut. I greeted the shop owner's wife, who, as usual, held the door open for me. Music played through one AirPod, and my mind wandered into the early evening. In a flash, out of the corner of my eye, I saw a man sprinting toward the same door I was walking to. Then, with tires screeching, two cars pulled up fast. Men jumped out of the cars, guns blazing. I didn't have time to think—I launched myself and the woman into the barber shop.

I was hit with three bullets: one in the chest, one in the left leg, and one that tore through my right femoral artery. I hit the ground hard, and there was blood everywhere. I didn't so much feel pain, but a rush of adrenaline and confusion.

The woman, the shop owner's wife—a mother of three beautiful daughters—held my wounds shut, staunching the blood with as many barbering towels as she could grab. Even in my disorientation, I realized that she was trying to save my life just as I had saved hers. We were in it together.

Then, in a moment of clarity, she handed me her phone, and I called my mom. When she answered, I blurted, "Mom, I've been shot. I love you, and I'm going to be okay—but I needed you to hear it from me first."

Before I could hear her answer, a police officer took the phone away and started triage. In the end, the tourniquet he applied saved me from bleeding out. I survived, but as I lay there on that floor, consciousness fading in and out, one thought kept playing in my mind: *If this is it . . . Am I proud of what will be said about me at my funeral?*

The answer was a devastating no. In that moment, I made a silent vow. *WHEN I wake up tomorrow, I will never live passively again. I will build a life so real, so purposeful, that if I ever face death again, I'll go out with peace— not regret.* That promise gave me enough energy to keep fighting—for myself, my family, and everyone I knew I was going to impact with my second chance.

Long before the bullets, I grew up an athlete—baseball and hockey were my arenas. They taught me how to win, how to lose, how to show up when everything hurt. I learned early on how to fight through pain, how to shake off failure, and how to keep skating when your legs were burning. Resilience wasn't something I learned later—it was forged in those cold rinks, long summer doubleheaders, and the hours upon hours I spent in the lab working to improve.

Still, by twenty-three, I'd drifted from that drive. I was working as a consultant. I had recently closed a multi-million-dollar deal just months before the shooting, which was a pretty big deal for someone my age. I made decent money and lived for the weekends—drinks, girls, parties, repeat. I thought I was doing what young guys are supposed to do. And if I'm being honest, I was good at it.

I had dreams—starting my own business, chasing physical challenges—but I kept them quiet. It felt safer to bury ambition under another round of drinks than to face the fear of trying, failing, and even worse, being judged by my friends. The funny thing is, I didn't even know I was stuck. I thought that low-level dissatisfaction was just how life felt for everyone. That "being stuck" was normal.

But getting shot ripped the sleep mask off. Suddenly, I wasn't trying to be cool—I was learning how to walk again. In fact, it's hard to "be cool" when you can't even go to the washroom on your own. I was told I might never walk normally again, let alone run. I was humbled in ways most people will never experience.

It felt like everything I had worked for was being challenged. Every workout I had done didn't matter when I lost forty-five pounds from bed rest alone. Every training session felt meaningless—because I might never be an athlete again. I knew for sure that I didn't want to survive just to sit on the sidelines of my own life. I wanted to *live*—for real. So I quit my job and threw myself into rehab.

Physical therapy and mindset work consumed me. I went for runs in the middle of the night, through the most dangerous areas of my city, just to scare myself into realizing getting shot was an anomaly, not the norm. I realize now that this was my own exposure therapy. Learning to navigate pain that didn't just hurt—it defined me. I drained my savings to give myself a shot at something better. And slowly, I started to rewrite my story.

Every time I defied a doctor's expectation, I realized something big: the limits people place on you are often just reflections of their *own* fear. Most "impossible" things are only impossible because no one around you has done them yet. But those people aren't you.

Within two days of entering the hospital, I made the call: I wasn't just going to walk again—I was going to run a marathon. Within one year. No one would've blamed me if I didn't; I had bullets in my legs, scar tissue wrapping key muscles, a broken femur, one hundred and forty stitches and staples in my legs, severe nerve damage, broken ribs, and bruised lungs. I didn't have a coach or a perfect plan, but I had a sense of clarity and fire.

In the beginning, the training was hell, and I limped through pain. I doubted myself often, but I kept showing up. I ran—or hobbled—my first 5K just ten weeks after being told I'd never run again. Quitting just wasn't an option for me. I needed to show the people I loved that I was going to be okay. More than that, I needed to prove to myself that I could still write my own future. There were moments I sat in my car after a rough training day, legs throbbing, unsure if I could even stand up again. I tried to cry. But I couldn't. I was too grateful for the chance to keep fighting to be sad about how scared I was. I stayed in the game. Not just for the finish line—but for the man I was becoming.

Today, I live differently. My life isn't perfect—but it *is* intentional. I run a consulting agency that helps small businesses and nonprofits unlock growth through digital marketing and AI tools. I build, teach, and problem-solve—on my terms. I founded a charity to help other trauma survivors, where we both mentor survivors and cover rehabilitative costs for those who need it. I am giving to other trauma survivors what I know is missing from a healing and recovery process that is very, very hard.

I ran my first Ironman five years after the shooting. Now I'm chasing my second, hoping to qualify for the world championships.

Since the shooting, I've worked with big name brands. I've spoken on stages to hundreds. I continue to reach tens of millions of people through social media. But what I'm most proud of? Being a shining light of hope for others who are told they may never—fill in the blank.

I don't waste time. I value the people I love. I invest in what matters. Some seasons, I grind. Others, I recharge. But whatever season I'm in, I show up with everything I've got.

Now, this is what I know for sure: you don't need a bullet to wake up. You don't need trauma to make a change. You just need to get honest with yourself.

You know what you should be doing. Even if you're bad at it. Even if you're scared. Even if you're "too busy." I've seen multimillion-dollar business owners work twelve-hour days, train for Ironman, and still be present with their kids. I've seen spinal cord injury patients grind in rehab all day and then show up for their daughter's dance recital. We all have more time than we think when we manage it properly.

The difference between a victim and a survivor is the stories we tell ourselves. I chose to stop being angry at the men who shot me. The moment I woke up, I realized: every second I spent focusing on them was a second I wasn't investing in becoming the man I wanted to be. Growth is hard. Getting shot is hard. But stagnation? That will kill your soul.

We remember our best days and our worst ones, while the average ones fade into a blur. So, I say, build a life full of meaning—where you take advantage of the blessings and the curses, and savor the little moments in between. Train for the thing. Start the business. Make the call. Forgive someone. Show up. Choose action over apathy. Choose effort over ease. Choose courage over fear and embrace this beautiful, messy, luminous life. If I can do it, so can you.

"Now, this is what I know for sure: you don't need a bullet to wake up. You don't need trauma to make a change. You just need to get honest with yourself."

8
MY LOVE LETTER TO DRUMMING:
Journeys of Rhythm, Courage, and Community

Lorenzo Jones

This letter is my attempt to express the boundless joy, love, and gratitude I feel for you—a companion who has danced with me through every chapter of my life. From the earliest whispers of your melodies in my childhood home of Evansville, Indiana, to the deep, resonant thrum of drums beneath an African moon, you have been both anchor and sail, guiding and propelling me forward.

If I had to trace the sinuous, pulsing line of rhythm that runs through my life, I'd begin with a single heartbeat—the steady, grounding sound of my djembe drum from Ghana. That drum, with its weathered wood and sun-warmed skin, became my closest confidant. In every hollowed tone and bright slap, I carried home with me. So, where and when did my love of music begin?

Years before, the heartbeat of music pounded in my blood, shimmered through stained glass, and echoed against the polished pews of Zion Baptist Church. My family's footsteps and whispered words hovered just above the hush, but it was you who slipped straight into my soul and never left. It was here that I learned that music and community are inseparable.

Attending church was not merely a ritual—it was an expectation, especially to sit up close, to be present, to surrender to the spirit. My mother, siblings, grandparents, and I would gather, forming a quiet constellation in the front rows, all eyes lifted. Yet, while the world around me demanded stillness, my heart thrummed in secret anticipation of the music that was soon to come.

The Pastor was a figure of both authority and artistry, each syllable released with such intention, as if he sculpted the atmosphere itself with his cadence. I watched, utterly mesmerized, as his words floated—weightless, careful, yet brimming with life—lingering in the air just long enough to become part of me. He would pause, his voice a gentle tide, and in seamless transition, the choir would rise. In that exchange, I learned rhythm was not just a beat but an elegant passing of the torch from one soul to another.

The organ—oh, how its pipes would swell and sigh, threading the sanctuary with strands of melody so sweet I sometimes wondered if angels were humming along. The bass, deep and resonant, planted its roots in my chest, grounding every word and note. The drums—steady and certain—marked the passage of time, each measure a heartbeat, each fill a reminder that life itself moves in patterns and pulses. Was it the movement of the hands that grabbed me or the way it made people move?

I was six years old, hands barely big enough to slap the skins of my first Bongos. Those humble beginnings were more than just playful experiments; they were the opening notes to a lifelong symphony. Years later, my mother, working part-time as a waitress in a jazz club to support us, unknowingly became the orchestrator of my early musical world. I would tag along after her weekend shifts, my young ears wide open to the spontaneous conversations of saxophones and the gentle murmur of upright basses. The dimly lit room vibrated with the energy of improvisation, and I was hooked.

It was there, amid the haze of cigarette smoke and laughter, that the club owner noticed my fascination. Perhaps he saw a spark—a silent rhythm pulsing through my veins—a mirror of the longing I didn't yet have words for. Out of kindness (and maybe a bit of hope), he gifted me a six-piece drum kit. That drum set was my passport to the world of percussion: the sharp slap of snare, the shimmering echo of cymbals, the thumping heartbeat of the bass drum. Each piece resonated with possibility, and I spent hours immersed in their voices, learning that music is a language spoken with both hands and heart.

At eighteen, I left Kansas, my family, and the familiar embrace of home to begin adulthood in Los Angeles—a leap into the unknown, driven by a hunger for self-discovery. The city in the early eighties was electric: a patchwork of cultures, sounds, and dreams. Venice Beach is full of roller skaters. Hollywood was filled with tourists during the day and partygoers and adult escorts by night. While I pursued my studies in fashion, the real education happened on dancefloors and in sun-soaked streets. Southern California's beach culture was a novelty, but I—this young Black boy from the Midwest—found my soul's nourishment in the city's music, not its sand.

No matter the venue or the hour, my friends and I would congregate wherever the music called. The laughter and the good company were woven together by the thrum of basslines and the syncopation of drums. As I matured, the rhythm—the pulse of the drum—grew ever more insistent within me. It was a call I could never ignore.

The true crescendo of our love story, though, arrived unexpectedly. Years later, I was invited by a wise, magnetic woman named Bettie to attend her three-day advanced transformation workshop. I sat in the front row, devouring every word, every concept, as if gathering kindling for the next great fire of inspiration. At the end, I approached her and confessed, "I want to hang out in your brain and learn more from you—you've exploded and unleashed inner gifts I didn't know I had." She paused, then offered me an invitation: "I go to Ghana every year and run a nine-day version of this training. I would love for you to come with me. I get asked all the time, but I've never taken a young Black man who could be a mirror for the young men over there."

Without hesitation, I said yes. Though I had traveled abroad before, I had never been to Africa—the cradle of my ancestry. The trip was transformative in ways words can barely capture. Our days were filled with intense, meaningful work supporting our students in expanding their worldviews of how they saw themselves while unlocking new beliefs, yet it was the nights I cherished most. There, among people for whom music, dance, and performance were not mere pastimes but vital expressions of being, we sang and danced as a group every chance we got. It was a moment of profound feelings of belonging. The air pulsed with the call of the djembe and other African drums. Their sound was ancient yet new, echoing in my chest and awakening something deep and true. It was as if I was hearing a melody for the very first time.

I remember walking down the dirt road with a guide when we came across one of his friends who had the most beautiful-sounding and looking djembe I had ever seen. The sound was mesmerizing as he moved his hand across the soft skin of the drum. The connection was so powerful that, without a second thought, I gave away the shoes I was wearing in exchange for a drum—a tangible symbol of the night music claimed its place at the core of my being. That instrument now sits among my most treasured possessions, its skin forever echoing those first heartbeats heard across the ocean.

MY LOVE LETTER TO DRUMMING ~ Lorenzo Jones

For years after leaving Ghana, the djembe was my anchor during moments of joy and sorrow. I'd play alone in my room or sometimes with my wife, letting each rhythm tell stories of distant markets, bustling festivals, where joy and laughter flowed like a steady stream. Yet something essential was missing—a call and response, the electric give-and-take that only emerges when hands strike skin in unity. Drumming had always been, for me, as much about community as about music. It was not enough to play; I needed to play with others.

That all changed the day I discovered my drum circle tribe in Oakland, California. It was serendipitous that my wife had a friend who performed every weekend at the local drum circle. At her invitation and suggestion, I summoned my courage to make the trek across the bridge to this community that was foreign to me. My heart pounded, my heart beat in a nervous, syncopated rhythm—with anticipation (and a hint of nervousness) as I arrived for the first gathering. My wife accompanied me, sensing the importance of this moment, and sat quietly beside me at the back, her presence a gentle reassurance.

I hovered at the edge of the circle, my djembe cradled in my lap, a swirl of questions in my mind. What kept me from joining immediately? Was it the unfamiliar faces, the fear of not belonging, the uncertainty of whether my skills would measure up? Each doubt played its own rhythm—a syncopated pattern of anxiety and hope. So, that first evening, I settled just outside the circle's embrace, listening and playing softly from a distance. Yet even from the periphery, I felt the magnetic pull of shared rhythm, the way a single beat could ripple out and encompass everyone.

Over time, with gentle encouragement and the warmth of the group, I found the courage to enter the circle. I still remember the first time I let myself be seen—truly seen—by these fellow percussionists.

My hands trembled, but my spirit soared. The circle wasn't about competition; it was about conversation. Each drummer brought a unique voice, a distinct story, and together we built something larger than ourselves. Slowly, I moved from the back row to the front, not just as a participant, but as one of the lead percussionists. In that space, surrounded by dancers, tourists, and locals, I felt alive in a way I hadn't in years.

Drumming in the Oakland circle became more than a pastime; it was a lifeline. The energy of the crowd, the swirl of dancers with their feet pounding the earth, and the smiles exchanged in fleeting moments—all of it nourished not only my soul, but the souls of everyone present. We became a community of healers and storytellers, each beat echoing with purpose. I learned that drumming could bridge worlds—between strangers, between cultures, between the past and the present.

Perhaps the most profound lesson was that courage is cumulative. Each time I entered the circle, I shed a little more doubt. Each time our rhythms locked in, I felt the boundaries between performer and audience dissolve. The power of the drum transcended language and background; it spoke directly to the heart.

With time, my passion for drumming led me beyond the familiar territory of the circle. I was invited to join a local Improv Playback Theatre group, a company that used music, movement, and storytelling to create performances from the lived experiences of the audience. Here, drumming became an even more fluid art—responsive, adaptive, and deeply collaborative. My rhythms underscored moments of grief and joy, suspense and revelation. I learned to listen not only to the actors, but to the subtle emotional shifts in the room, letting my hands translate the unspoken into sound.

Drumming with the Playback Theatre troupe brought new challenges and delights. There was no script, no set pattern to follow—only the pulse of the moment. I came to love the uncertainty, the creative risk of improvisation. It demanded presence, vulnerability, and trust in my fellow performers. It also rewarded me with a sense of connection unlike any I had known before.

Looking back, I see that drumming has always been my teacher. It has taught me patience as I learned new rhythms, humility as I listened to others, and resilience as I faced setbacks. Most of all, it has given me community—a family forged not by blood, but by shared experience.

When I reflect on my journey, I am grateful for the lessons I have learned, both at the edge of the circle and at its heart. I am grateful for the courage that allowed me to move forward, for my wife's steadfast support, and for the many hands and hearts that have joined with mine along the way.

Drumming is more than music; it is a way of life. It is a language of joy and sorrow, of longing and belonging. It is a reminder that, even when we feel alone, there is a circle waiting for us—a place where every beat matters and every story is honored.

So this is my love letter to drumming: thank you for carrying me across oceans and into new friendships; for teaching me to listen, to risk, to lead, and to follow; for reminding me that the truest rhythms come not from perfection, but from the courage to play, together.

May the circle always be unbroken, and the heartbeat of the drum continue to echo in every corner of my life.

*"Drumming is more than music; it is a way of life.
It is a language of joy and sorrow, of longing and belonging."*

9
LEARNING TO LOVE WORDS AGAIN

Deana Kitajima

The sting of hot tears in kindergarten was my first inkling that something about my brain was fundamentally different. I loved words. I loved the way they felt on my tongue when I spoke them, the rhythm of sentences, the stories they wove. Yet, the simple act of writing them down, especially getting the spelling right, was painful.

My great-grandmother and great-aunt lived far away, and writing letters was our family's cherished tradition, keeping us close. Every year, a birthday card arrived with a lengthy birthday wish and a handwritten check for $2. It was my custom to reply with a heartfelt thank-you letter, detailing how I'd spent my small fortune. I relished this ritual, filling pages with notes and drawings, until kindergarten introduced a new, confusing rule: misspelled words were no longer okay.

My lovingly crafted letters, complete with artwork, were suddenly returned to me, decorated with stinging red circles that identified mistakes. My dad would try to soothe me, reminding me that they loved me more than anything. But the weight of knowing their love and the feeling of profound shame was too complicated for my small self; words got choked up in my throat, and tears rolled down my cheeks every time.

The pressure escalated by third grade. That's when we learned that math, too, was an uphill battle. I wrestled endlessly with my multiplication tables, a crucial skill for fourth grade. The news that my upcoming teacher was a "stickler" for math facts hung over me like a dark cloud, intensifying the pressure to get a jumpstart over the summer. I certainly did not want another year of criticism and disgrace.

That year, I spent the summer with Great Auntie Orielda and Great Uncle Bill. I loved them dearly, and they were willing to devote time to teaching me what I needed to know for fourth grade. My excitement was boundless: I was eager to finally learn my multiplication tables, and I was going to ride a train for the first time in my whole life. Most excitingly, I was going to see my Auntie's turtle refuge (she rescued and harbored more than a hundred desert tortoises) in her giant backyard hobby farm, a place she lovingly called her sanctuary. I would also learn all about Uncle Bill's extremely rare and extensive coin collection while learning math.

Unfortunately, it turned out to be the longest and most painful summer of my life. It is true that when I first arrived, I loved everything. I loved telling them all about the train ride as we picked delicious and juicy cherry tomatoes from the vines. I loved the smell of my auntie's car; it literally smelled like "time" to me. I also loved riding in my Uncle Bill's pickup truck, going to the farmers' market with the windows rolled down, and getting to choose any vegetable I wanted for dinner. I also loved going antiquing with him after the market and trying to learn math. Trying to learn how to count my change back to him, trying to learn the difference between a one-dollar bill and a one-hundred-dollar bill, and trying to add up all of the receipts when we got home.

It was in all of this "trying" that they realized they weren't going to be able to teach me by letting me do fun things. That's when my Auntie had a brilliant idea. We cut open brown paper sacks and laid them out flat so I would have a giant sheet of paper to work on. Each paper was to represent a set of multiplication tables.

This was so fun for me, cutting the bags, laying them flat, and anticipating all of the learning I was going to do at the kitchen table! At first, it was fun for me to write out all twelve number ones in a long perfect column, and then all of the times table X's in a column next to them, and then each number—one through twelve—in the next column, followed by a column of equal signs. This was kind of like art to me, and I loved it! I already knew the one times tables by heart! Everyone knows that one times twelve is twelve.

It was when we moved onto all of the other tables that I knew the fun was over. To this day, it is very hard for me to say the word "multiplication" without feeling queasy. When I struggled to memorize my two times tables, we moved from the paper method to flashcards. Eventually, the tears came rolling down my face, and I was sent to my room. Soon it was decided that I should utilize the brown paper and rewrite repeatedly, the tables with the answers; surely I would remember the right answers by then. Also, by moving this task into my bedroom, I could work at the desk, a small writing table in the corner, with no distractions. My "easily distracted" personality was something that seemed to disturb my Aunt, and she had grown tired of it.

Staring at the paper, trying to force understanding, required my brain to take frequent, involuntary breaks. When I was isolated in my room, there was no way to control this essential process. I needed daydreaming more than ever; I felt like my room was a prison, and dreaming was my escape.

Although this daydreaming mind made it possible for me to feel less alone and less anxious, I didn't accomplish the task in the amount of time I was given. This really enraged my Auntie. She threw her hands in the air and said, "That's it! You are your Uncle's problem now!"

To my delight, I got to move from my writing table to Uncle Bill's worktable in the garage. I loved that garage and time with Uncle Bill very much! He let me tinker with things as he told me stories and asked me questions that made me see my dreams develop as if we were playwrights, and this garage, full of wonderful relics and antiques, was our stage. One by one, he told me cool stories about history and wove into the story a number and its significance. One story I remember so vividly is all about the Forty-Niner gold rush era. I was fascinated! Growing up in a small town near Hearst Castle, I knew all about mining and the significance of hard work and big dreams.

It was thrilling when he said, "So, since you are such a smarty pants and you listen to every detail, what are those miners called?"

I shouted out with confidence and joy, "The Forty-Niners!"

He laughed that signature belly laugh of his, picked me up off the table, and twirled me around! "That's Right! That's exactly right!" He said it over and over as he lifted me in the air and spun us around. I can still see and feel the joy as he gazed into my eyes and gave me his giant smile.

When he sat me back down on the work table, my favorite place to sit because it gave me a bird's-eye view and I could dangle my feet and swing my legs, he said, "Guess what?"

I looked at him with big eyes for the next surprise. I remember that nothing came out of my mouth; I was hanging on in anticipation for the next part of the story. I leaned into him as if to say out loud, "What?" and he leaned into me and he said real steady, "You just learned what seven times seven is!"

I realize now that Uncle Bill instinctively taught me in a way my neurodivergent brain could grasp: through narrative and multisensory engagement, making the information meaningful rather than just relying on rote memorization. He didn't just teach me facts; he breathed life into abstract numbers.

As time wore on, the challenges of learning got more and more difficult. The assignment load was always far more than I could manage within the allotted time. Reading was a constant uphill battle. They told me I couldn't read, but I knew I could; I just needed what felt like an eternity compared to my peers. During the summer between fourth and fifth grade at Girl Scout Camp, I quite literally forced myself to stay in my tent, away from all distractions, to prove it. Slowly, painstakingly, page by page, I devoured Beverly Cleary's *Henry Huggins and Ribsy*. I loved that book and still do.

Although my grades were always far below average, I kept moving along. By the time I reached Mr. Harrah's College Counseling Office, it was clear my grades wouldn't get me into Cal Poly, the college of my choice. The good news, he told me, was that Cuesta College was a gateway into Cal Poly, and this became my path.

Just a few days after that meeting, I was called back into his office. He had done a favor for me that I can never repay. He had called the YMCA and recommended me as a student counselor. There was one thing I had to do, and he would prepare me for it. I had to go for a job interview. He walked me through keeping my nerves at bay, how to greet the people in the office, and how to answer some of the possible questions. I was set.

The day I met Annie, the day of the interview, was a life-changing and transformative day. She hired me on the spot and then explained that there was one problem we had to address before I could start when summer arrived. We had to request a waiver from the state of California for my age because I was younger than the average junior in high school. Annie believed in me so much that she went out on a limb for me. I was so honored and grateful. That summer job convinced me that children and education would forever be part of my life. I breathed differently that summer than I ever had before. I was alive more than ever before. I was happier than ever before. I was in my element and thriving!

College changed my life. There, I met my best college friend, Donna, on my first day of Nutrition Class, and we remain friends to this day. After one day in English 1A, I headed back to the Student Learning Center. For the first time on my own, I had to say out loud, to a stranger, that I had a hard time reading and writing.

During one visit to the Learning Center, I was told that a person named Cheryl would be interested in talking with me if I was open to it. I booked a meeting with her, of course, because I needed to know how I was going to get through my classes. Cheryl explained to me that she suspected I had something called dyslexia. She said I may even have dyscalculia. In order to see if I had these two learning disabilities, I would have to come back for another appointment and go through a series of tests. If I did, in fact, have dyslexia, they offered a program built on a newly developed curriculum called the Lindamood-Bell method, which could help me. Hearing this gave me a feeling of hope, and I am so very thankful I was encouraged to keep exploring learning possibilities for myself.

It turns out I do have dyslexia—several forms—in addition to dyscalculia and dysgraphia. I now know this makes me "neurodivergent," a term I never knew could apply to me. It's such a beautiful word to me now. It's like a kaleidoscope. It gives so much more room for the different shades and colors that can be seen on the spectrum. I'm fifty-six years old and just now understanding this. How can this revelation have possibly taken so long?

The answer is complicated. Neuroscience has come a long way since 1968, the year I was born. Also, terminology has changed, diagnostic tools have changed, and the number of brave people who openly talk about their disabilities has increased. I believe the more we know about something, the better we can understand it. The better we understand it, the better we can accept, support, and embrace it. One of my missions in life is to make sure that people know they are loved. It is in this getting to know myself, learning to love myself, that I have found the greatest love of all.

"It turns out I do have dyslexia…I now know this makes me "neurodivergent," a term I never knew could apply to me. It's such a beautiful word to me now. It's like a kaleidoscope."

10

BORN FOR BLISS

Lisa Martin Naimi

As an intuitive healer for sixteen years and painter of soul-inspired images, I have evolved in stages along the ascension path. Amazingly, the healing and awakening process activated divine downloads of heightened awareness and sacred rituals within me. As I evolved, the programs I now share awakened a hidden archetype within me: The Artist. I now work with energy workers, healers, and yoginis as they discover their path to personal mastery.

Seven years after my awakening, a gateway to a higher level of consciousness dawned upon me with a swift and decisive force. At first, I was terrified, feeling my "consciousness" leave my body, and in that impenetrable darkness, I struggled to find a focal point of awareness. Often, my response to utter darkness in every direction was despair.

Suspended in that inky nothingness, a dark silence swallowed the promise of light, and I prayed for escape. Frantic, I searched for the boundary of this hollow realm, an exit, an egress, or another point of awareness. I discovered that if I struggled, the enormous nothingness responded with more nothingness. "I am alone," I told myself. And then, a lifeline realization: "Oh f*ck, I need help."

Well-versed in the rituals of self-care, I attend my standing weekly appointment with my mentor. A chiropractor, acupuncturist, and clairvoyant energy healer, Anne supports me to heal physically and spiritually while activating my spiritual gifts and supporting me to remember my greater self. When I reported my consciousness-nothingness predicament to her, she studied me and then responded, "I'm just trying to figure out where you are!?"

She doesn't know what to do for me or how to help me ground into my body, I thought. The feeling of nothingness continued in every direction.

As I came to accept my unusual circumstances, half of my consciousness returned to my body and I existed in a bewildering, identity-shredding split-state for ten days. For ten days, I lingered on the edge of dissolution. For ten days, I was suspended between my body and The Void. For ten long, bewildering days, I wandered lost in a spiritual darkness, seeking solace and finding only more emptiness.

I ambled through my life, feeling the strange disconnection between what I came to think of as a polarity of Thingness/Nothingness. Ordinary objects felt simultaneously solid . . . and ethereal. It was as if my fingers sensed the energy field of each cup, each picture frame I touched, even the texture of the air I breathed. Impressions came and went. I was aware of a connection to Source, which then dissolved into the liminal space between thoughts. For ten days, insights found me, then fled, only to return again. It was an agonizing game of peek-a-boo.

I was able to care for my basic survival needs but couldn't tolerate deep conversation or process any kind of "ordinary" information. I was consumed by the Thingness/Nothingness of everything. When not managing daily tasks, the unending vastness of The Void loomed as a focal point. Each moment in The Void was spent searching for an exit. I grew increasingly worried that this was a new normal state from which there was no escape.

Day ten dawned just like the previous nine. At last, exhausted, I stopped wrestling with my consciousness, stopped dancing with the howling fear. Completely drained, I gave up. With nothing left to resist, I surrendered. I surrendered to The Void.

In the moment of surrender, love found its way into my consciousness. The constant tension between my heart and throat eased. The twisted cramping in my belly relaxed, and I could feel the tension of fear melt away. That was the moment I let love in. A burst of freedom, expansiveness, and bliss consumed my awareness. I returned to wholeness and fully awakened consciousness in this body.

Relief followed Surrender. Peace eased into contentment. Freedom flowed into relaxation. Consciousness found relief, releasing any need to focus, to connect, to entrain to anything at all. All I needed to do was float in The Void, just BE. Nothing weighed on me or bound me. There was only, ultimately, peace.

I sensed I could return to the Void, at will, at any moment. The Void revealed its gift of respite from the constant stream of the 60,000 or so thoughts that rise up daily in the normal human consciousness. I recognized The Void as a space of awakening, which invited me to return again and again.

It called me to explore my humanness and the expanded nature of human consciousness. In this space, a state of oneness arose. I sensed I was in tune and merged with everything and everyone. It was as if we were one being. It was always fresh and new, and eternal. The Void was a paradox of extremes and balance. It offered a sense of wholeness and felt as if it was the center of everything, where all co-existed in an unmanifested state.

Now, as I center my awareness in The Void, I simultaneously feel my particles expand outward into its expanse. It feels as if I might dissipate into the Nothingness of endless expansions. Rhythmically, as

I breathe, particles flow inward, particles flow outward in a lemniscate (figure eight or infinity) pattern. I notice the particles return to my center with a momentary sense of relief.

A mantra arose in those moments of awakening: "I AM the Void, I AM the Void, I AM the Void."

In this space, I sensed my particles co-mingling and exchanging with the particles of others sharing the space of The Void with me. Even now, as I write these words, I feel The Void inviting me into its embrace. Love has been trying to get my attention for as long as I can remember, inviting me deeper into the expanse of creation where my awareness dwells in The Void.

Two years later, my awareness dawned within the Holy Womb of the Divine Mother. This was the fifth in a series of teaching moments. Each time a mystical vision invites me into its embrace, my consciousness leaves my body, and I forget about this life on Earth now. Peace infuses my point of awareness again. In contrast to the Void experience, invisible movement in the pattern of the infinity symbol dances in every direction simultaneously within the boundless emptiness. Bliss dances through me. Yet, the emptiness now has consciousness. Bliss consumes me. Infused with the satisfaction of existing in this nowhere-place since the beginning of forever, I know I will continue infinitely. The enormity of this thought carries a sense of being far greater than my individuated consciousness. It's as if I am remembering that I AM Source, and Source is me, as we all are. I AM Bliss.

In this fifth initiation of deep awareness, a golden-white rod of light flew toward my center with great intent. I heard myself ask, "What is that?"

A disembodied voice responded, "It is LOVE!"

The rod of love energy connected with the core of my awareness, and instinctively, I spiraled myself around it like a snake. The moment my spiral-snake form reached the far end of the rod, every potential exploded into manifestation. With my next breath, I returned to my physical body and full-awakened consciousness.

After this sacred initiation, Anne and I returned from a weekend of offering our healing and intuitive reading services at the Sun Valley Wellness Festival. Throughout the weekend, one of Anne's colleagues regaled us with tales of Braco, a European spiritual healer whose gift of silent gazing inspires international crowds to attend his events.

Later, Anne and I met at her office for my weekly appointment. As she began the healing session, I was aware of a subtle and translucent male figure standing at the foot of Anne's massage table.

"Anne? Do you see what I am seeing?"

Anne's eyes fly open. "Yes!"

I was aware that the man was communicating with me. I sat up, and he gave me a message for Anne. "He is offering to give you the ability to heal through gazing. Would you like that?" I asked.

She nodded vigorously and whispered, "Yes!"

I recognized him as Braco, in his lightbody form, and watched as he performed an energy healing for Anne and activated the gift of gazing within her.

Early in our relationship, Anne had confided in me her belief that she was an incarnated angel. With tears streaming down her face, Anne fully extended her arms from her shoulders, and I could see translucent wings unfurl from her back.

When the transmission was complete, Anne turned to me and asked, "He says it is your turn. Would you like the healing ability of gazing, too?"

Eyes streaming, I nodded my head in the affirmative. Braco moved across the room to me and began the same upgrade on my energetic field. When the healing and activation were complete, I was aware that Braco had cleared the path from the Cosmos, through my crown chakra and into my heart, to allow the love of the Divine to anchor into and flow through me. It's as if I were feeling real love for the very first time.

I have come to understand an awareness of my Higher Self through the unfolding experiences of my spiritual journey. As I dismantled decades of cultural and familial domestication, my authentic self began to shine through years of accumulated distortion. Much like the journey of the ancient Sumerian goddess Inanna, who resurrected after a voluntary descent into the Underworld, I recognize that my Higher Self guided my personal resurrection, helping me restore my sense of sovereignty.

I now know myself as a mystic healer and visionary artist who surfs the quantum waves of multi-dimensionality. I navigate universal consciousness with a flexible belief system, which I can only describe as a living river to source that opens gateways and allows me to reclaim my blueprint of Self as a fractal of Source. I have become my radical, radiant Self.

Looking back on my transformation, I now see that what began as bliss within the Divine Mother's womb evolved into a confrontation with my shadow. It started with an experience of personal loss that was a preview of global change. While the development of my spiritual gifts began to evolve as early as 2007, it wasn't until 2019 that a series of experiences rocked me to my core. A five-year dark night of the soul challenged me to grapple with a sense of abandonment by the Divine Mother, of both friends and family, until I could no longer justify or rationalize distorted or abusive behaviors in myself and others.

My ten days in The Void was an initiation. By courageously facing my core wound head-on, my soul created space to heal. Instead of investing my energy into tending the needs of others, I turned inward, where the hidden archetypes of Artist and Writer blossomed.

In that accelerated timeline, exploring my spirit changed how I self-identify. Mental health counseling changed my self-expression. I adopted tools to identify distortions, healed traumatic patterning, and established healthy behaviors. I used both mysticism and counseling to access the expression of my whole self.

Of course, the Divine Mother hadn't abandoned me. That was just my brain making sense of the upheaval and pain coursing through me. Working in concert with Her, my Soul and Higher Self led me through a deep Underworld journey of release, enabling my rise as my sovereign Self. All along the way, I encountered allies and tools that built a foundation of self-love and respect. According to Daniel J. Schmidt, founder of the Awaken The World Initiative, when our awareness awakens to the next layer of consciousness—when we really level up—all of the unresolved unconscious material below that layer rises into the awareness for healing and resolution.

After all of these revelations, I ask myself, "What is my larger story?"

And then I remember a process my Persian husband (now a U.S. citizen) shared with me. Sayed shared that while growing up in Iran, the poetry of Rumi (a 13th-century Persian Sufi mystic and the best-selling poet in the United States) was an oracle for insight.

I asked Sayed for his help, and he offered me the choice of two books. I chose *Rumi: Fountain of Fire*, by Nader Khalili. I closed my eyes and asked my burning question, "What is my larger story?"

I paged through the book and tuned in to my empathic senses. The energy pouring down through my crown chakra, body, and legs guided me to the page I needed. I handed the book to my husband and listened intently as Sayed read the following passage:

"Rumi's greatness has to do with... the most essential message of traditional religion everywhere: Human beings were born for unlimited freedom and bliss, and their birthright is within their grasp. But in order to reach it, they must surrender to love."

It's been a journey to this point, and it will continue. I now know that the journey is infinite, and Surrender to Love is a path to Mastery.

11

SAINT TOBIAS:
A Love That Bridges All

Dawn Airhart Witte

In Hawaiian culture, you do not call yourself your pet's "owner." You are referred to as their *Kahu*. The word *Kahu* has a deep meaning and is defined as the sacred role of guardian, protector, steward, or honored attendant. Essentially, someone entrusted with the safekeeping of something precious, something cherished. What a Kahu protects is not their property. What they protect is a part of their soul.

I am a four-time foster failure, a *Kahu* whose heart has been claimed by every animal I've ever met. Since I was 18, I have been a sanctuary for 17 dogs (one I rescued from Puerto Rico), 23 cats, bunnies, mice, fish, a tortoise who's been with me for more than 20 years, and squirrels, including my beloved Sammie. I've thrown two monkey birthday parties and visited sanctuaries to connect with creatures of all kinds.

My daughters often joke that they were raised in a zoo, and they pretty much were. I wanted them to grow up surrounded by animals because animals teach us what no human ever could: unconditional love, compassion, and the truth that love is a language all souls understand. As a child, I would cry to God about hungry animals, longing to feed them all, and that ache has never left me. It is a calling, a profound love for animals that I have felt deep in my soul for as long as I can remember.

One of my favorite memes captures this love perfectly: "If you ever hear I was killed by a mountain lion, know that my last words were, 'Here kitty, kitty'."

It's a half-joke, but it speaks to the fearless devotion I have for every creature. A quote I hold dear says, "Until one has loved an animal, a part of their soul remains unawakened." I have felt that awakening over and over, through every furry heartbeat that's joined mine. Each animal has been a blessing, a teacher, a piece of my heart. They have brought joy beyond measure, and grief that cuts just as deep. Losing them has taught me life's hardest lessons, but also its most sacred: love is eternal, and it is what matters most.

Among all my cherished babies, one stands out as a love for the history books: Saint Tobias—Toby, my little man, my monkey, my tiny dog, my perfect baby. A Pitbull-Great Dane mix, Toby, came into my life after I lost my beloved Whitney and Lola, both Great Dane-Pitbull mixes. My dogs and cats have usually been rescue animals, but my daughter had found Bentley, our 11-year-old baby, through Craigslist, and after Whitney and Lola passed, I felt a pull to do the same. I typed "Great Dane/Pit Bull mix" into the search bar, trusting God's guidance, and there he was—one listing, one miracle. The moment I saw him, I knew he was mine.

Toby was not just a dog; he was my ardent protector, my shadow, my Velcro boy. He did not sleep next to me—he slept on me, his warm eighty pounds a constant comfort, as if he couldn't bear to be even an inch away. I never liked leaving him, even for the shortest time, and he hated it when I left, his soulful eyes pleading for me to stay. I used to half-jokingly say we were codependent, but everyone knew it was true.

Maybe our souls knew we would only have a short time together, just under three years, and we had to soak up every moment we were given.

I often wondered how my young Toby would grieve Bentley's loss, given Bentley's age and the fact that Toby LOVED Bentley so much. I never imagined Toby would be the one we would grieve first.

A few weeks ago, my almost three-year-old little man passed away after a brief illness—an undiagnosed autoimmune disease that stole him far too soon. To say this took me by surprise would be an understatement. I was not ready to lose him; I do not think I ever could have been. When he took his last breath, I was by his side, whispering "Mommy loves you," my heart shattering as I held him. If grieving could bring him back, I would wait forever, but sadly, life does not work that way. There are holes in my heart that will never be filled, but I am grateful for every moment I had with Toby—every snuggle, every chase with Bentley, every time he looked at me with those eyes that saw straight to my soul.

The human part of me wants to ask why. I prayed, my beautiful friends prayed too, but he passed anyway. I believe in the power of prayer, but I have also learned to trust God's plan, even when it breaks my heart. Sometimes we question God when we cannot understand why things happen, but I have come to see that surrender opens us to miracles we might otherwise miss. The day Toby passed, I went to Craigslist, searching for Great Dane/Pitbull mixes, just as I had when I found him. There were no listings, and I thought, "This is not the time to look for another dog who needs a home."

But the next day, I woke up with a pull to try again. This time, I did not search for dogs—I just clicked on "pets," and the second or third listing said, "Rehoming dogs and puppies." I opened it, and there it was: Great Dane mixes. I took it as a sign, a whisper from God, the universe, my angels, Toby, and all my animals who have passed, guiding me to a new baby.

I contacted the person, asking if they had any little boy puppies. They did, and after a few emails, they asked me to meet at a gas station. I went with my friend Portia, my soul daughter, who was visiting from Ohio. We stopped at the wrong gas station, but when we looked up, the sign read, "Extra Mile." Portia always says, "The extra mile is never crowded," a mantra we share about going above and beyond for others—being the person we wish we had, whether for a stranger, friend, or family.

The irony was not lost on us as we sat at an Extra Mile gas station, waiting to meet the puppy. The man arrived, opened his trunk, and said, "I brought two."

Before I could even think, I blurted, "Can I have them both?"

They looked just like Toby—black-and-white Great Dane mixes, doppelgängers for my little man when he was a baby. I knew they were not Toby, and they would never replace him, but I had not expected two puppies, let alone two that looked so much like him. I knew they were meant to be in my life.

I named them Saint Thomas, meaning "twin," for his striking resemblance to Toby, and Saint Theodore, meaning "gift of God," because they truly are. I have seen them sleeping in poses that mirror Toby as a puppy, and in those moments, I feel him near. I know God, the Universe, my Angels, and all my animals, who I have loved, helped me find these two new babies. If I had not been open to following my heart, I would have missed exactly the puppies I was meant to have. God answers prayers, sometimes in ways we do not expect, and this was one of those miracles—a reminder that love endures, even through loss.

There is something so special, so divine, about the bond between humans and animals. We speak different languages, but we understand each other through our hearts. The moments I have shared with my cherished babies have been the most beautiful and heartbreaking of my life. Just the other day, I was talking to Thomas and Theodore, asking what kind of nonsense they would bring into my life. I started listing my dogs, beginning with Bentley. When I said, "Jakey brought nonsense," Teddy came up behind me and took off my hair scrunchie. Jake, another of my cherished babies—dubbed "The Golden Boy" by my daughters for our super-special bond—used to do the same thing when he was a puppy. In moments like these, I am certain the love I have shared with each of my babies lives on. We are always connected, bound by love that transcends time and space.

Toby's love, and the love of all my animals, have taught me profound lessons that I carry with me every day.

First, it taught me to surrender to what life brings. I used to miss the miracles in life, but surrendering—trusting God's plan, even when it hurts—has shown me that the universe always has a beautiful plan. What we put out comes back to us, often in ways we cannot predict, like the arrival of Thomas and Theodore.

Second, it taught me to cherish every moment. No one is promised tomorrow, and when we are fully mindful of this, we understand the value of every second. I miss Toby and will for the rest of my days, but I would not trade a single moment. My daughter, who drove seven and a half hours to be with me and Toby, sent me these lyrics from a Taylor Swift song the day Toby passed about a little boy who died: *"What if I really thought some miracle would see us through/ What if the miracle was even getting one moment with you?"* That's Toby—every moment with him was a miracle, a gift I will hold forever.

Third, love has taught me that we are connected to all things. The Vedic text, the Katha Upanishad, says, "The self is not born, nor does it die." I believe this—our souls are eternal, and love is the thread that binds us across lifetimes. I know Toby and I will find each other in every lifetime, and when we are not physically together, our love will always be there.

Fourth, it taught me that life is sacred. Every being—human, animal, even the bees I save—has a soul worth seeing, worth loving. *Sawubona*—I see you—is how I live, and it is how I honor my animals' sacred lives.

Finally, love has taught me why we are here. Love is the greatest elixir, the universal language every being understands. While we allow race, religion, politics, and gender to separate us, we forget that love is the bridge between us and everything. It is why we are here—to love as deeply as we can, for every moment we are given.

With great love comes great pain, but that pain is a small price to pay for the gift of love. When Toby passed, I asked him to let me feel him—not his physical presence, but his essence. I immediately started crying, and that was my answer.

As Rumi said, *"Tears are prayers too, they travel to God when you can't find the words."* Love helps heal broken hearts, even when they are broken into a million pieces. It is the only thing that can. We think we have time, but we never know. I used to always tell Toby he was too much—his enormous personality, his constant need to be on me, his boundless love that filled every corner of my life. But as my friend often says, "When we plan, God laughs," and I could not help but smile when God sent me two—Saint Thomas and Saint Theodore—doubling the love and mischief. 'So, two it shall be,' I thought, trusting the divine timing of this unexpected blessing.

Love is the most important thing we will ever have in our lifetime. It is the only thing that matters, the only thing that lasts. Make decisions about love from your heart, follow its pull, as I did with Thomas and Theodore, and as I do every day with Bentley, Sammie, Tortoise-Tortoise, and all the souls I have loved. Let life flow through you. Cherish every moment, every heartbeat, every scrunchie stolen by a playful pup. Love as deeply as you can, for it's the bridge to everything—past, present, and future. That is what Toby, my little man, taught me, and it is the legacy I hope to share with the world.

12
FEROCIOUS COMPASSION

Sandra Bargman

I bought my first piece of artwork when I was twenty-six. I was living in Tokyo at the time, fulfilling a ten-month contract working at Tokyo Disneyland, performing in two of the theatrical shows that ran daily. It was an extraordinary opportunity for me to have the time to delve into Japanese culture, which I seemed to know and feel viscerally. The park shows were fun, the Japanese cast members were exquisitely talented and professional, and I, as a result, had my snobby "I don't do theme park" conservatory-trained ego delightfully smacked down.

One day, on my day off, I took myself on a solo adventure into downtown Tokyo. After a long day filled with shopping and sightseeing, I meandered into a second-floor art print shop, with cabinets galore filled with gorgeous woodblock prints. I was overwhelmed by the variety, colors, and sheer number from which to choose. I looked at many that day, but I purchased the very first print I pulled out: "The Girl Taking Off the Smiling Red Mask".

I remember the tears that sprang to my eyes when I first saw that print, standing in that crowded, dusty shop in Tokyo. I knew I was that girl with the red mask. And once you know something, once it takes root, you cannot stop knowing it. I longed to take the mask off. The mask of the good girl, the mask of the people pleaser, upbeat, sugar and spice, and everything nice.

I began my acting career in my first play when I was six years old. I don't remember the name of the play, nor my character, but I do remember having an epiphany during our performance as I stared out into the spotlight. Being on stage felt more like real life to me than my actual life. People pleasing was simply another style of acting for me. It is a performance that I create every day, whether or not I'm aware of it. And of course this is true, for my mother, and her mother, and all the women in my life.

People-pleasing is rooted within the patriarchy, and the roots have grown deep. The social obligation that tells people, primarily women, to make themselves small in order to cause less trouble. This leads to frustration, resentment, anger, and depression. I was a prime example, always waiting for the "right" moment to speak, downplaying my accomplishments, incessantly apologizing, and perpetually accommodating. Back then, I didn't even know how to express anger or sadness, let alone depression. No, back then, I developed an addiction to nicotine, to swallow and "smoke screen" my emotions. As women, we are often not socialized to reveal anger at all. How many of us hide behind this mask?

What causes this anger? Well, ask 10 women and there will no doubt be 10 different answers. But I know all the answers will meet at the intersection of self-betrayal. When did I begin to betray myself to be liked, to fit in, to avoid confrontation, and most horrifically, to feel safe?

I came into this world with the belief, the knowing, that I was here on Earth to contribute to Life.

My mother told me that when I was around the age of three or four, I walked into the kitchen with my hands on my hips and announced I was "here on a MISSION." I knew I had something to say. I'm sure you did, too.

But also, I was destined to learn the well-known and demoralizing story of "Too Much." Too loud. Too bossy. Too self-confident. Too sensitive. Too needy. Too pushy. Too crazy. For the record, I have been called all of these. I am unapologetically all of these, according to those in my circles for whom my exuberance for life, my powerful presence, and self-confidence have been a trigger.

I was raised by parents who came of age in the 1950s, when girls were sugar and spice and everything nice. My parents were the quintessential good parents, the good daughter married the good son, prone to following the rules, side-stepping confrontation, and embracing the tribal suburban myth. Our house looked like every other house, with our dandelion-free manicured yard, basketball hoop, and backyard grill. We fit in, and we kept up with the Joneses.

My mother was my best friend and greatest fan, and I lived her unrequited dream of performing. My father, angry at his own parents, tossed aside his natural rebel spirit for parenthood and took his anger out on my burgeoning creative and preternatural ability to communicate. It was all there in my DNA. The good girl and the angry rebel. Therein lies my mission. And my trauma.

In the late 1990s, my husband and I visited my parents during one of their vacations in Asheville. Family friends and a cousin lived nearby at the time and joined us for brunch at the famed Biltmore Hotel, built by George and Edith Vanderbilt as a private home—a time-traveling treat for all of us.

After our feeding frenzy, we went for a walk across the street alongside some abandoned train tracks. My cousin and I fell into conversation about our latest work opportunities, and we moved ahead of the group. Then, the conversation turned, focusing on what was then a new cultural phenomenon: reality television, and my cousin waxed rhapsodically about this new style of entertainment.

Finally, he turned to me, perhaps because I had fallen silent, and asked, "What do you think of reality TV?"

I paused. This moment is etched in my memory. I made a decision. "Do you want my honest answer?"

"Of course."

To people-please or not?

"I think it is the lowest of low vibration spectator entertainment, redolent of gladiator sport. Moreover," I said, warming up to speaking my truth no matter how his face grimaced with distaste, "It's childish, cruel, and will have severely detrimental ramifications on society." Hyperbolic perhaps, but nonetheless exactly how I felt.

He called me condescending.

Because I didn't agree with him, because what I said rang true to him, despite his enjoyment of it, and I am certain this truth felt like an attack. It wouldn't have mattered what I said if he were stable in his self-assessment; however, he was not, and he instantly became offended, childishly playing the victim. The short conversation was twisted into a conflict rather than a simple difference of opinion.

I burst out laughing. Something had shifted. An insignificant conversation, certainly, yet monumental. After years of longing, I had chosen to dislodge the red mask.

Interestingly, reality television is a quagmire of people-pleasing. Contestants or cast members may voluntarily refrain from expressing their true thoughts or feelings, even if they disagree with others, to presumably avoid conflict or disapproval. Contestants are desperate to please and not be cut, to be overly concerned with pleasing others, seeking validation and affirmation through their actions and words. You just can't make this shit up.

And in the epic irony category: How utterly predictive was I? We've elected a reality television administration who have enamored a cult of people addicted to reality television drama. Every news cycle seems to contain a new episode of chaos orchestrated purely for ratings. Alas, New Yorkers always knew what a reality TV "loser" he was, to coin a phrase of his.

Speaking of the city, my hometown of choice, as a professional actor, I've probably pounded more pavement than the average New Yorker. Many years ago, I started a classic NYC experiment while I was out bobbing and weaving the busy streets of midtown.

One day, I simply stopped moving out of the way of people I was passing. If someone didn't move out of my way, we would bump into one another, sometimes quite hard. If this did happen, part of the experiment was to keep moving with no acknowledgment. Unsurprisingly, never once was it a female with whom I slammed shoulders; no, it was 100 percent men.

As any good New Yorker knows, being kind is very different than "being nice." What is that old phrase? "The East Coast is kind but not nice, the West Coast is nice but not kind." And as an empath, I am keenly aware of my inclination to take on people's pain, in an effort to help, but always to my own detriment. My job is to know what's mine, and that's a full-time job.

But as a woman in a patriarchal world, I have been indoctrinated with people-pleasing. Perpetual people-pleasing is the source of much of my anger throughout my life. In ways large and small, from allowing others to interrupt or talk over me, to not standing up for myself for fear of being branded too emotional or aggressive, to leaving a job due to harassment. And it's this very anger that has kept my heart closed, a form of self-punishment. The journey out of people-pleasing has been a long road marked with a lot of shoulder slamming.

Finally, the day arrived. It was a couple of weeks before the US presidential election in November of 2024, and I was driving on a red and gold fall afternoon, chatting on the phone with a childhood friend. After inviting my friend to my home upstate, I concluded the conversation with:

"Unless of course, you vote for him, in which case you aren't welcome in my home." I could feel him stop breathing.

"What?" he said, finally.

"You heard me. You can't vote against my human rights and the rights of the people I love and expect me to welcome you into my home."

There it was. It landed with perfect precision.

For the record, "He" is simply a representation of our collective shadow, and I refuse to give him too much credit for what has been established as a decades-long campaign to "reclaim" the patriarchy—at all costs.

I told my friend I would always care about him, and when and if we saw each other, I would offer him a loving hug.

But there was no way that I was going to make any effort to play nice and empower him to feel comfortable with his choice to align himself with a regime hell bent on taking away the rights of women, people of color, the LGBTQ+ and Trans communities. It was a line in the sand I was, as it turns out, quite comfortable drawing.

As an Interfaith Minister and someone who is devoted to understanding myself as a spiritual being having a human experience, I like to believe that I'm a bridge builder. The word 'compassion' gets bandied about in all my circles. Originating from the Latin *compati*, compassion means to see the suffering of others and take action to stop it. While this is a noble pursuit, it leaves much room for interpretation. The choosing and taking of actions can also be filtered through ego, control, and judgment.

My highest spiritual understanding of compassion is this: Allow everyone, without judgment or hatred, to make their own choices on their own path. Think about the profound and life-altering generosity in that.

Ferocious Compassion requires that I find the courage to speak my truth, to find the courage to be disliked, to find the courage to turn and face confrontation. Ferocious Compassion guides me to choose authenticity over approval. My friend has the right to make choices for himself. Ferocious Compassion allows me to make mine, for my own highest good, and not for anyone else's comfort. It allows me the freedom to assert myself, to be vulnerable, to express my true emotions and intentions.

For my own heart to stay open, I can no longer pretend to "make nice" and try to understand the numerous assaults on my intelligence and my integrity. I can no longer befriend people who vote against my reproductive or equity rights. I can no longer tolerate cruelty, anti-intelligence, and belligerent racism.

I truly saw to whom and with what he was aligned, and there was absolutely no explanation that would make it palatable. I am exhausted, and am no longer willing to allow the bitterness to creep in. I want my heart to stay open and loving despite being broken because we can't just shut down our hearts for one situation. Once we shut down our heart for one thing, we shut it down for all things.

I will meet you where you are, seeing you for who you are while maintaining my own boundaries. This is why I choose the word ferocious. It fully embraces my anger, transforming it into self-care and protection. I am reclaiming my wild self, my power, and authenticity. 'Ferocious' is dangerous, and so am I. My kindness and open-heartedness are ruthlessly courageous and free. I am no longer able to self-contort to fit in, be liked, or make others comfortable. I don't want to help women be strong. I want to model ferocity.

#FerociousCompassion is self-respect and self-care. It is a love note to me. What lies beneath the mask? The freedom to be me.

13
BIRTHING THE WILD FEMININE WITHIN

Esther Wyss-Flamm, PhD, E-RYT

Body take me deep
Down into the knowing
Of the mothers who walked before me.
That I may sit at their feet,
Listen to the ancient tales,
Taste the broth of their bones
Cupped in the sacred palms of this earth.

~ prayer I wrote after a miscarriage

Growing up, I stalked the stacks at libraries, a voracious reader of myths, fairy tales, and sagas. I loved climbing trees, running across open fields, and listening to music in a cluttered basement with my friend Maggie, who lived next door. At night, I lay sprawled out on the driveway, leaning into the warmth of our dog, and stared up at the stars.

I had dreams that landed me in intricate plots featuring freakish monsters and magical forces that protected me. One of them took me underground into hollows among the roots below, to find a cave guarded by an elder woman stirring a giant cauldron of bone soup over the fire. She ladled some of the simmering soup into a bowl and handed it to me. I ran away. The ancient wild feminine was terrifying; decades would pass before I could make peace with this part of me.

Over time, I started to walk past the climbing trees with low-hanging branches; Maggie went away to boarding school; and I forgot to gaze at the stars. I was preoccupied with homework, wanting to "be normal," and later with a career in social change organizations. Starting with the U.S. Peace Corps, this work took me (and a few years later, my partner Bradley and I) to far-flung places overseas. The horizon in front of me felt wide open and exciting.

Which brings me to the moment when I was sitting in the cracked pink bathtub of our home in Lusaka, Zambia, where Bradley and I were living at the time.

I lay surrounded by soothing, warm water, precious water. Drought was a factor at that time in Southern Africa, so it felt indulgent to draw a warm bath that afternoon. I watched a thread of red blood flow out between my legs—the dark color blending into the clear water in wisps and swirls, as lifeblood met Life Element Water. Tears streamed down my cheeks as I lay in the tub in the sweet embrace of warm water on my skin, knowing that I would release the kernel of life that had died deep inside of me. Tears turned to sobs, my eyes gazing up at the branch of the guava tree outside as it knocked against the window.

All I could do was release and let go into the moment. And the moment meant that the pregnancy I had held for three and a half months was now sliding out of me. I knew the sadness was real: the joy and secret feelings of wanting to hold a sweet-smelling baby that I'd carried in my body dissolved here in this moment of blood meeting water. My back was aching, my cramping was intense, and I felt vulnerable and scared.

That's when I heard words in a voice that I didn't yet know coming up inside, a female voice, telling me: "Listen to your body, it knows what is coming. You are not alone. Trust that your body knows what it needs. This is a time to let go." And here I was, with a soft, clean cloth beside me, letting gravity do what needed to happen. I felt her voice and then her presence guiding me, telling me to breathe just a moment longer. This was what I had fought hard to deny for days, keeping my legs tightly wound together, ignoring the bloody streaks that had appeared on my underwear, making light of the fluttering cramps.

She went on to tell me: "Stand up, Esther, it's time to stand up." I stood, and a clump of blood and tissue slid out of my body into the palm of my hand. I placed it on the soft cloth. Later, I wrapped up the cloth and put it into a small box that I placed under the bed.

In the coming days, my sadness turned into anger and frustration: I told myself that it was time to move on and get rid of the box. Once again, that reassuring, serene voice returned to bring me the deeper clarity I needed: the box was to stay where it sat under the bed.

I lay despondent. Only I knew it was there, the little box of a dream interrupted. While I was aware of what had happened clinically, another part of me sought a deeper understanding through fleeting images that appeared in my dreams.

A few days later, I sensed her guiding me to go bury the box outside by the giant elephant ear leaves under the guava tree. This felt real and right. I was able to stand up again and felt strength surging up inside. I was able to reconnect with Bradley and face the world around me.

Still, unfriendly thoughts developed in my mind: how could I have messed up this most fundamental part of being born female? A deep mistrust of my body, a sense of having been failed, began to settle in. These perceptions were reinforced by comments from family and friends: "miscarriage has never happened in our family before," and "all I have to do is touch my husband's underwear and I end up with a baby nine months later."

It was at that time that I noticed the power of sitting in stillness. When I sat quietly at the beginning of a day, even for just ten minutes,

I could breathe freely. I observed that those judgmental thoughts weren't real, that they were fabrications of my mind. Then I felt better in my body and could move on with my day.

Life flowed back into its rhythm, I dove deeper into my job, and the voice that had guided me through these difficult months receded. I noticed a shift: the work was no longer as satisfying. A year later, Bradley and I decided not to renew our contracts and began graduate studies in the midwestern United States. I was soon pregnant again. Yes, I told myself, the stars are aligned this time, and I'll become a mom.

It didn't happen. The ultrasound at twelve weeks indicated there was no heartbeat. I was told that the pregnancy was not viable and that it would be easiest to get a D&C. One moment, I had a small orb of light and hope inside, the next, I was empty, the pregnancy vacuumed out of my body in a sterile hospital setting—I never saw it, never felt it flow out of me; no one could see it, it was just me and my invisible loss.

Throughout this time, the voice I had heard guiding me stayed disconcertingly quiet. And I didn't have a box to bury.

More cycles of miscarriage followed, punctuated by myriad tests for both of us, hormone injections, and a slippery slope of increasingly invasive interventions.

I hated the waiting room of the high-risk OB/GYN practice, walls plastered with baby pictures and heart-shaped thank-you cards. The doctor had a stellar reputation; he wore cowboy boots as he strutted from room to room filled with clients yearning for full-term pregnancies. For me, the process would run its course: after trying for months, I find out I'm pregnant, go in for an ultrasound, learn there was no heartbeat, submit to another D&C, and then try again.

That summer, I caught a glimpse of myself in the mirror of the lavatory of an airplane on our way to a family reunion, giving myself a carefully timed hormone injection. I saw a steely-eyed thirty-something-year-old woman, and barely recognized her. The drone of the airplane vibrated my body. I took a deep breath and felt a deeper, softer knowing take hold inside. Relief flooded through me as her voice returned to tell me: "This is not your path."

I was tired of trying to force something, playing games with my body, and tricking my mind.

In the months after I jumped off the fertility roller-coaster, I listened more closely to her voice. I noticed my connection to her grow stronger during that early morning meditation. My regular yoga practice also allowed me to get past the noise to discern something deeper within me, something that reminded me that all was already and always okay. The kind and gentle voice that occasionally rose to the surface during these times made it okay to dissolve into tears and feel my sadness.

Bradley and I wondered about the instinct-driven need for our genetic material to be part of a new life we'd bring into the world. Was this rooted in a desire to see my face in that of my child? In the end, the need for a biological connection didn't seem as important as wanting to parent a child. We decided to pursue adoption.

And we soon landed on a whole new mess of questions: Adopt locally? Nationally? Internationally? Interracially? We pursued an open domestic adoption, and a few months later, we were selected by a teenage couple to become parents to the interracial baby they were expecting. That opportunity fell through, as did the next one, when a grandmother showed up to parent the newborn. Our social worker urged us to consider international adoption, and after another nine months, a photo arrived from Vietnam: a tiny girl named Thinh wearing a frilly dress, looking up at the camera. She needed parents. Something rose up inside as I gazed at the photo. Hope does spring eternal! We said yes, and we sat, and we waited.

Thinh's adoption papers made their way through layers of bureaucratic review one slow step at a time. We waited past her first birthday, her first footsteps, her hospitalization with pneumonia, her move to a foster family, her entry into full-fledged toddlerdom. Six months later, we were notified we had less than a week to travel to Da Nang, Vietnam, to meet this little girl. On the wings of this promise, we expedited tickets and visas and endured sleepless nights at the hotel.

The morning after our arrival, we showed up early at the gates of the Children's Center and were handed a little wisp of a girl. Thinh looked as exhausted as we were. She struggled and cried when I tried to hold her. Bradley had more success; she allowed him to rock her to sleep in his arms.

The following day, we officially became Thinh's parents in Da Nang's city hall. We fell in love with this spunky, tiny toddler who ran away wherever we went, already set on taking off on her own. We named her Maya and flew back home as a family.

In the adoption community, there is much talk about the strength and resilience of love residing at the heart of this arrangement. But flying from the vibrant life we found in Vietnam to the stark midwestern winter, I felt heavy with the truth. Intercultural adoption meant that we were tearing Maya from her homeland, her context, and the language she was just learning to speak.

None of us adoptive parents likes to think too much about this side of the arrangement. We may work hard to build bridges with our child's culture of origin (honoring celebrations, cooking the food, and building relationships with a nearby Vietnamese community), but in truth, we chose a path our privilege and resources allowed us to take, and didn't look much past the tunnel vision of our deep desire to be parents. Who is to say that I would be the right mom for this bouncy toddler? How can we ever know? We trust, we love, we take it day by day, we believe, and hold on to each other.

The ease of our lives as a couple slipped away as we became Maya's parents. Our connection as a threesome became strong and steady. Those first weeks turned into months, and then a move to family student housing in California. Amid as diverse a community as one could possibly find, Maya grew and thrived. I remember her exuberance, a girl skipping with her Mom, riding on the bike with her Dad, commandeering monkey bars at playgrounds, and digging enthusiastically in our community garden, then sleeping heavily after a story at the end of each day.

We agreed that Maya needed a sibling. We had sent in an application to adopt a second child when I discovered I was pregnant. Sigh. I knew this path all too well. I felt a protective wall go up inside. I knew my body would again contend with cells coming together to form another being. This time, the knowing voice inside of me reminded me I needed to be present for Maya and the strong, determined energy she was bringing into our lives.

My body embraced the pregnancy during those first weeks, and the ultrasound let us know there was a heartbeat.

"That doesn't mean anything," is what I said to Bradley. "We've been here before."

"Let's not think about it," he said.

Asking a woman not to think about a baby growing inside her is like asking her to cut off her head—not possible.

My body started growing like the squash on the vines of the community garden outside. We cancelled our plans to adopt a second time. Maya became enthralled by "her" baby that would be arriving. Could I contradict her? No, I couldn't: it was her baby. As I pushed her "higher, Mama, higher!" in her favorite swing, I knew I would not be carrying a pregnancy to term without her vibrant presence in my life.

I felt myself release into the experience of growing a baby. The seventh month brought me a most exquisite and unexpected gift: I was visited by a dream of the Spirit Children. I saw four children running toward me on the horizon, waving. At first, I didn't know who they were, but then I recognized them as the Ones who didn't find their way into the world through me. They came close enough for me to see their smiling eyes. In West Africa, an area of the world I'd lived in for seven years, there is a word for Spirit Children: *abiku*, "those who are elsewhere waiting to be born." I woke up from this dream, feeling relieved and happy that they were nearby, so beautiful and fine.

Our son Theo was born in a natural childbirth with a woman named Luna as the attending midwife. At one point, she guided my hand to touch his crowning head between my legs, a fleeting moment of grace, followed by sensing him slide out of my body and then be gently placed on my belly. I drew him into my arms, an awkward bundle covered with tissue and streaks of blood, squinting eyes, and a mouth that soon found its way to my breast.

Over the course of seven years, my body drew me into a deeply personal journey of transformation. Learning to listen for wise guidance and access the wild feminine within taught me to surrender to the flow of life and death, to drop into stillness, to move and loosen the parts of me conditioned to be cerebral, driven, and goal-oriented. I can now draw on the fierce energy of the feminine to move more freely, connect with the Earth rhythms, ride waves of creativity, and savor the short time we have on this planet.

I close with an invitation for you, dear reader: What moments come to mind when you've sensed an opportunity to step into your deeper wisdom self? What might you need to release to allow the wild feminine to rise up and have space to roam in your life?

14

HOW I LET GO OF MY BREASTMILK AND FOUND FAITH

Leah Kahn

Standing in front of my fridge with my baby on my hip, I stared at the unopened bags of breastmilk, calculating how much I should give away. What if I suddenly stopped producing? What if it became difficult to pump at work and I needed to rely on my freezer stash?

Faith and I have never been the closest friends. Hypervigilance has. Strategy. Skill building. Independence. But faith . . . I leave that to my little sister, an expert at going with the flow who knows that it will "all work out somehow." That wasn't how I typically organized the world. I wanted to give a mom in need at least 100 ounces of breastmilk, but what if I ended up needing it one day? What if I suddenly stopped producing? Giving Hadar formula would not be a crisis, but I had become intimately connected to breastfeeding her and felt idealistic in my quest to make the experience last as long as possible.

I hadn't been sure how or where to donate my frozen milk. Sitting in a parking lot after a ballet class one Sunday morning, I contacted a milk bank. Then my friend connected me with someone who was looking for donations for her friend with breast cancer. Because this new mom had begun chemo just after her baby was born, she was seeking donations. Tears pricked my eyes as I read the text. I quickly got in touch with her.

Giving my milk to a family with acute needs felt good; and it felt equally magical that my body could help in such a primal way. After sharing with my husband that I found somewhere to donate it, he enthusiastically said, "donate all of it!" I smiled, but his unabashed enthusiasm triggered my anxiety. Could I depend on my body to keep producing at its current rate? I wanted to operate from a place of abundance, but I felt the weight of primal responsibility on my shoulders, and these considerations as a first-time mom left me with a new kind of vulnerability I hadn't previously experienced.

As I wrestled with these thoughts, I recalled our ancestors who were commanded by the mitzvah of terumah (an offering to God or a gift to another person) and offered korbanot (sacrifices that bring people closer to the Divine) to God as a symbol of the relationship between humans and the Divine, as found in the 26th chapter of Deuteronomy: "When you enter the land that the LORD your God is giving you as a heritage, and you possess it and settle in it, you shall take some of every first fruit of the soil, which you harvest from the land . . . put it in a basket . . . go to the priest in charge at that time and say to him, "I acknowledge this day before the LORD your God that I have entered the land that the LORD swore to our fathers to assign us."

The Kohanim accepted agricultural and animal sacrifices, acting as intermediaries between the community and the divine. But what is interesting is that upon arriving to a new land, the people of Israel are immediately commanded to sacrifice their agriculture—even in a place where they are not yet established.

But that is, of course, the point, "Were not the mitzvot given so that man might be refined by them? Do you really think that The Holy One of Blessing cares if an animal is slaughtered by front or by the back of the neck?" Bereishit Rabbah 44, reminds us. "Therefore, mitzvot were only given to make humans better."

In other words, bringing sacrifices to the Kohanim and, ultimately, to God, affects the giver. Fulfilling the mitzvah might not demonstrate a person's inherent courage or faith but going through those actions might cause them to develop courage and faith. In essence, people flex their spiritual muscles by engaging with the commandments, which can lead each person to become a more evolved human.

Additionally, the Kohanim worked on behalf of the community and weren't able to own their own land or cultivate agriculture, so they depended on the generosity of the community to bring them closer to God and fulfill their responsibility to engage in the work of the Temple. Today, since we don't have the Temple, prayer has replaced sacrifice, so we offer our hearts to the Divine through our words. This, too, teaches us about the spiritual underpinnings of sacrifices.

We might think the sacrifices are simply about the items being offered, but they are more than that; spiritually, they're about offering up ourselves. And this offer of oneself requires a great deal of faith. I realized that the act of giving away my extra milk was probably the closest spiritual experience I could have to understanding what b'nei Yisrael must have experienced during Temple times: giving from a place of abundance even when I could never be certain I would have enough.

I decided to act with faith as my central motivation. I felt the need to verbalize what I was about to do, so I pointed to the bags and explained to my ten-month-old baby that we had worked together to produce this milk, that another baby really needed it, and that we were going to give it to her. When Kate showed up at my door to collect the milk, I dutifully put 16 bags, totaling 160 ounces, in her cooler. As she left to bring it to the mother in need, I thought about the countless episodes of *Parenthood* and *Queer Eye* I had watched while pumping in my nursing chair—and the many emails I wrote while pumping at work. These all went with her.

I had put real work into producing those bags of milk, but I didn't realize at the time that the avodah (spiritual work) of keeping my child alive and nourished would actually become more vibrant when I helped someone else in need.

Becoming a parent had pushed me to find a faith in myself—and others—that I'm not sure I had before. I have transformed my ability to be pushed past my edge, and in that pivoting, I've increased my capacity to negotiate predictable and unpredict-able moments alike. I've learned that when answers aren't clear, wisdom will come, the next step will be revealed, and I'll know what to do.

Closing the cooler, I suddenly understood the declaration scripted in the book of Deuteronomy, proclaiming the roles of God and humans in the process of creation, in which humans are invited to participate. When the Israelites would offer up their first fruits, as part of the choreography and drama of the moment, they would say "I acknowledge this day before the Lord your God that I have entered the land that the LORD swore to our fathers to assign us."

It might appear that the point of this declaration is for God's sake, but I think it is actually for the human engaging in terumah, to clearly mark the completion of the mitzvah. The statement is an act of radical gratitude, both acknowledging the constellation of events necessary to arrive at this moment and paying tribute to the ecosystem that enabled it to happen.

Because the Torah's commandments inspire us to undergo a spiritual process, we're enabled to respond when called into something bigger than ourselves. Thanks to Jewish tradition, I pushed my fears aside to reach a place of faith and achieve an attitude of abundance.

The character refinement I experienced with this powerful act led to a deeper understanding that I couldn't predict the future.

And so, our work for the moment done, I turned to Hadar, smiled and made my own declaration: "Hadar! Guess what we just did? We helped another baby! We donated our breastmilk!" She giggled, smiled and nestled her head into my chest. As Kate's car drove away, I felt grateful for this simple but transcendent lesson of faith.

"We might think the sacrifices are simply about the items being offered, but they are more than that; spiritually, they're about offering up ourselves."

15

MAKING MEDICINE FROM GRIEF:
A Story of Stillness, Suffering and Surrender to Motion

Jennifer Coffey

I met grief when the unexpected death of a loved one hit me like a cannonball. Prior to that, I had an intellectual understanding of suffering, a capacity for sympathy, a deep relationship with sadness, and flirtations with depression. I didn't truly know the sticky shape grief could and would take in my body. That cannonball opened a space in me, and grief filled it in like a dense and romantic fog.

Prior to that moment, I was working an uninspiring, unfulfilling full-time administrative management job in local government. In that role, I experienced workplace trauma that took residence in my jaw. It was 2007, and the concept of gaslighting wasn't as widely talked about or understood as it is in 2025.

I recall my boss saying something like, "You're so intelligent, but you seem to have a blind spot here."

By here, he meant the systemic fraud that I and other quality assurance colleagues across the state had uncovered and were about to shine a light on. The economy was tanking, and I had just purchased my first home. He actively made my work life miserable, reminding me about my financial responsibilities and how difficult it would be for me to find a new job. He told me to keep my mouth shut, kept me out of meetings, revoked some responsibilities, and piled on other meaningless circular work.

Given my Western view of pain from a purely physical perspective, I sought help from local dentists. At one point, the pain was so extreme that I pulled over in traffic on a major highway to call the nearest oral surgeon, begging them to remove my teeth. Since there hadn't been any physical trauma or bleeding, this doctor and others scheduled me for an exam and couldn't find anything wrong or a reason to extract teeth. The jaw pain persisted, and the mental stress was relentless.

An acquaintance passing through town at that time listened to my woes and invited me along to a weekend meditation retreat. This was a new concept to me. Again, my Western orientation couldn't comprehend the rationale or reason to pay money, drive somewhere remote, sit still, not talk, and expect my jaw pain to disappear. What I ultimately experienced that first weekend and in the days, months, and years that followed was that through conscious breathing, a gradual quieting of the mind occurred. It felt like mental gymnastics, trying to weave through the busy bus station of thoughts and feelings, and just put my attention on my breath. Counting helped. In the early days, I rarely got up to 15 in-breaths and 15 out-breaths before my mind was back on the topic of my maniacal boss and the system I'd found myself stuck in. It was work to notice that I got off the counting bus and got on the misery bus. It was also work to not punish myself, to stay with it, to keep going back to one in-breath, one out-breath. I'd have to actively redirect myself back to the breath-counting bus and away from the suffering bus. Both buses were coming by, and it was my choice. This was a new and revelatory concept. Noticing these thought patterns gave me space to experience life in a new way, where I could be in choice about which emotional or mental state I let lead me. I was giving the power of choice to forces outside my body, such as my boss or the state of the economy.

What makes me and people like me susceptible to these outside forces is a topic for a deeper dive at another time. These thought patterns, relationship patterns, and emotional triggers have roots and branches. Up until this point in my life, I was just looking forward into the future without introspection or self-reflection. Metaphors were just metaphors. Stories were just stories. Dances were just dances.

With meditation practice and conscious breathing, I began to experience the science of rewiring my brain and being in choice about my thoughts and feelings. Neurons that fire together wire together and so forth. It was a new seed, and it needed to be watered and tended to grow and change the mental and emotional landscape. I began to have the lived experience of the gardener metaphor, and the bus rider who chose the bus of less suffering.

Over time, breath by breath, I released the tension I was holding in my jaw. I was holding. I released. I took control of the bus station and all of the buses. I learned that suffering is at the root of the dharma teachings, and taking in those stories allowed me to be with the history of my own pain and experience it in the context of a universal human experience, which connected me to all life around me since the beginning of time.

For example, when I hear a story, my imagination pictures it, and my emotional body feels it. Breathing in and out, the posture of the great bodhisattva of compassion, Avalokiteshvara, as I contemplated my own female form in a state of self and universal compassion. By making this mental shift, I was able to see my role in creating, holding, being with, releasing, and letting go. Just like the bodhisattvas, and weary life travellers on this bus ride before and after me. One breath at a time, I was helped by witnessing, hearing, and embodying the stories of those who came before me, by taking in their experience, wisdom, and allowing it to be a guide for my own unique version. I found a fulcrum of life balance through weekly Insight Meditation community dharma talks and group sits.

At the first tea break, I recall someone asking me, "What brings you here now?"

After a long inhale and exhale, I condensed the big story down to one word. I simply replied, "Suffering."

"Oh, yes. That's why we're all here."

The pain in my jaw lessened over the months and years. Thanks to my direct meeting with suffering through that job, tempered by meditation practice and community, I felt my young adult self growing into a new level of more measured maturity.

Three years of regular meditation practice created shock absorbers for the sensitive skin-and-bones suit I moved through life in. It also added rearview mirrors that showed me the history of human suffering and love through the lenses of many cultures and eras. I was beginning to catch glimpses of a peaceful and calm version of myself in the mirror of the present moment.

I had just accepted a new job with the hope of more fulfillment when the cannonball of grief tore through me, leaving a gaping hole where all of the peace and calm disappeared. I experienced a level of soul and body pain that I had not known before, and it was beyond mind. The peaceful comfort and stability that sitting meditation had provided was no longer available. When I tried to sit quietly, the grief would rise up in me, and I couldn't contain the howls.

This medicine had expired, and I was unable to renew the prescription. I did not want to empty my mind of the truth of this death, this loss, this grief. I didn't want to inhale and exhale it away. For the next nine months, there were moments when I wanted a break from the grief, but I felt like it would not let go of me. I would put my body through the morning routine and waft out the door, off to work, only to return home and be pulled down to my knees, sobbing into the living room rug, piles of tissues like clouds in the unrelenting fog.

Much as I tried, I couldn't THINK my way out of grief. I needed some way to continue along this human path fraught with suffering, when seated quiet meditation was no longer an option. After a while, when people offered words of condolence, I found myself replying, "You gotta dance while the sun is shining." I felt the profound gift of life, and whether I knew how to handle it or not, I had it. Without any thought, that little saying became a mantra and a lifeline.

In the years since that first meditation retreat, I availed myself of a variety of personal growth workshops, including Gestalt, holotropic breathwork, and vision therapy, to name a few. It was in a 5Rhythms Heartbeat workshop that I discovered a new blueprint and keys that I never imagined possible. I was clumsy, I didn't consider myself to be a dancer, and knew nothing about the origin of the practice when I signed up. I gave myself permission to leave the workshop if I didn't feel up to it and would consider it a success if I only put one toe on the floor. I needed a way to navigate through the fog of grief. I knew what the problem was, and talking about it didn't change it.

Grief was my passport to "dance."[1] Grief was the outfit I wore. God, source, the universe, whatever you call it, was directing the dance. I was willingly at its mercy. I was in awe of how it moved, how it danced, how it shook, how it trembled, and yearned. When I fully surrendered my skin and bones to grief, along with my heart and mind, my entire body and being to be moved and breathed until it exhausted itself, fell to ashes, and rose back up again and again and again. The grief and I changed shapes, transforming constellations of real and shadow histories, dreams, and stories of family, friends, lovers, neighbors, allies, protectors, ancestors, teachers, jesters, threats, perpetrators, saboteurs, demons, and an unending matrix of possibility. I felt safe enough to go deep into the pain and let it move.

The 5Rhythms map offers vast lifetimes of landscape for unending exploration. I sought out conscious dance practice spaces and attended weekly sessions without making eye contact or speaking with other dancers for the first two years. It was my grief therapy. It was my personal healing practice. I tuned into the energy of the space and danced with the projections and shadows, reliving and revising histories, plans, and dreams. Grief held me in place like a dance partner in the fog, with a hazy view of past, present, and future. Once I was able to open my eyes and ears to the other dancers, the macro experience, if you will, the container transformed. The fog of grief began to dissipate, and I could meet the others in the present moment. I had space for their truth, while also leaving room for the great unknown mystery. No longer completely consumed by grief.

The shapes and rhythms that have moved through me over the years are now tools and medicines that I initially gathered haphazardly, and later with care and precision. Dance workshops became my travel itinerary and provided community in motion through time zones. I met the Movement Medicine® mesa (map) at a workshop in Germany and felt immediately in love with the practice, the form, the structure, and energy holding of the space. Soon after, I moved through Movement Medicine initiation workshop, apprenticeship, and professional training with clarity. I was exactly where I was meant to be, completely in the present moment of my life, rarely sitting still.

I now carry an apothecary born from lessons learned, suffering stewed, joy ignited, love unbound. Now 12 years into my practice, I can sense when the truth of my story in movement is read by another. For example, on the dance floor, I may cast my eyes down, with full vision of the space around me, shake my hips to the rhythm, and tune into my womb. In the early days and years of practice, I did this unconsciously. Now, more than a decade into my practice, I consciously invite a conversation, a circle of stories if you will, with the other wombs in the space. The wizened ones, not needing permission, usually get the invitation first. They come in all ages, shapes, and forms. They bring their wombs close and tune in, greet each other in motion, acknowledge each other, listen deeply, while the hips roll, shake, and cradle. There is a meeting, a deep knowing. In making my dance visible, I offer permission and invitations to those present to witness, to know my story, and risk telling their own.

I know when I have been seen and understood by someone in a way that only the body knows, and the mind lacks vocabulary for. There is an energetic knowing, a communication that is simpler and more complex in its definition and understanding, only told body to body. This womb-to-womb dance is one of many story forms. Is it the story of ecstatic lovemaking? Conception? Birthing? Breaching? Bleeding? Longing? Vacating? Grieving? Withering? Resting? I don't know, and I know all at once. This is the language of the body in motion, containing every possibility, pouring out as needed. This is the medicine I carry now—not from being completely consumed by or erasing grief, but from moving with it. From taking the time to listen for the body's stories, and trusting that they, too, hold the medicine of universal language and transformation.

---

[1] I use the word "dance" as shorthand when referring to forms of conscious dance stemming from 5Rhythms, including but not limited to Soul Motion, Open Floor, Azul, 360, and Movement Medicine.

"In making my dance visible, I offer permission and invitations to those present to witness, to know my story, and risk telling their own."

16

SOUL NOTES

Sheherazad Barnes

My deepest earthly connection as a child was with my grandmother, a devout Muslim woman whose faith was woven into every moment of her life. Five times a day, she would retreat to her prayer room, and often, she would invite me to sit with her as she prayed. I would mimic her movements, bowing and whispering in reverence, though I did not understand the words. I did not need to understand the words to feel their power. The room would fill with a palpable presence, a sacred energy that shimmered like sunlight on water. I could see the light around her as she prayed, a radiant halo of devotion and grace. She attempted to teach me to read the Quran, but while the words did not take root in my mind, their vibrations etched themselves into my soul. I knew, even then, that I was witnessing something divine.

I was blessed with a vivid connection to the unseen. To the world, I was an only child, though I had a brother and sister much older than I who had already begun their adult lives. My parents, socialites immersed in their own world, entrusted much of my upbringing to nannies and caretakers. But I was never truly alone. My days were filled with conversations with my "imaginary friends," beings who were as real to me as the earth beneath my feet. They were my companions, my confidants, and my protectors. They tucked me into bed at night and accompanied me wherever I went. I felt wrapped in a cocoon of love and light, guided and nurtured by an unseen presence.

And yet, as I grew, the connection to my unseen friends began to fade. I do not remember when they stopped visiting or when I stopped noticing them, but life carried me away from that enchanted realm. For many years, I wandered, disconnected from spirit, consumed by the demands of the material world. I pursued a career in fashion and, by all outward measures, was successful. I earned a comfortable living, but inside, I was empty. My body grew weary, my soul sick with longing for something I could not name. I longed for more. I knew there had to be more to life than slinging the perfect pair of jeans or styling the next big trend. Deep down, I felt my soul was meant for something greater—to leave a legacy, to make a difference. I could hear the whispers of something beyond, but they were so faint, drowned by the relentless hum of modern life, the pressure to succeed. In the fog of ambition, I barely discerned the call of my soul, yet a quiet longing gnawed at the edges of my being, refusing to be silenced. The endless hustle.

Then, about fifteen years ago, the call of spirit returned and became impossible to ignore. It was a loud whisper at first, then a persistent echo reverberating through my being. I found my way to kundalini yoga, and in those first few sessions, it was as if an ancient remembrance was ignited within me. Through the rhythmic breathwork, the pulsation of movement, and the chanting of the sacred naad, I felt myself transported beyond time. The echoes of the mantras reverberated through heart and mind, dissolving barriers I had unknowingly built. It was as if a forgotten language of the soul was speaking to me again, wrapping me in waves of light, and the spark of my sacred purpose was lit once again. I was plugged back into the divine current, the source of all life. In meditation, spirit returned to me. I heard the familiar voice, felt the loving presence, and saw the radiant light I had once seen around my grandmother.

This time, the light enveloped me. It filled every cell of my body, dissolving the walls I had built around my heart. I wanted nothing more than to swim in that light forever, to merge with the bliss that had been waiting for me all along.

Spirit guided me with unmistakable clarity: I was not living my purpose. I was meant to be of service. I was meant to share the message of Divine unity. I was meant to teach about the oneness that binds us all. The bliss I experienced in meditation was not meant for me alone. It was a gift to be shared, a reminder that we all have access to this divine channel if only we create the space and set the intention.

I immersed myself in study, deepening my practice of kundalini yoga and exploring various healing modalities. Reiki, pranic healing, sound therapy, and crystal alchemy bowls became my tools for transformation. The alchemy bowls, in particular, opened a portal to the mystical, their harmonics transcending the physical realm and carrying me to a place beyond time and space. Life became magical once more. Miracles and synchronicities abounded—not merely as fleeting moments of chance but as profound affirmations of alignment. When I was in flow, life unfolded with grace; the right people appeared at the perfect moment, opportunities materialized effortlessly, and *everything I needed found its way to me*. It was as if the universe itself conspired to support my journey, reaffirming that when you are aligned with your soul's calling, life becomes a dance of divine orchestration.

I felt held, guided, and supported every step of the way. Eventually, I left my corporate job and stepped fully into my role as a healer, transformational coach, and spiritual guide, leading retreats and sharing the tools that had healed me.

Then, as I reached a spiritual peak, my devotion was tested. Not long after I began to live in alignment with my soul's purpose and teach others how to do the same, I lost my beloved father, the man who had been my greatest source of strength, my inspiration. He was my best friend, my champion, and my guiding star. His death shattered me. I traveled to Seattle to arrange his funeral, a task that felt insurmountable in my grief. I stayed at my uncle's home, spending long hours in his small office, poring over old photographs and trying to find the words for my father's eulogy. On the desk in that room, I noticed a statue of the goddess Isis. I remarked on it to my uncle, surprised that he, an elderly man with no known interest in Egyptian mythology, would have such a figure. He explained that he had acquired it during a trip to Egypt many years ago.

Somehow, despite my grief, I managed to create a beautiful tribute to my father. After the funeral, as I prepared to return home, my uncle handed me a box.

"She wants to go with you," he said.

I hesitated, but he insisted. Inside the box was the statue of Isis. I carried her home like a sacred relic, guarding her as if she were made of pure gold. When I placed her by my bedside and removed the tag, my breath caught in my throat. The inscription read: "Isis, Goddess of Funeral Rites and Motherhood."

Though I had always associated this sacred deity with magic and resurrection, I had not known of her role in guiding souls through the passage of death. At that moment, I understood. She had been with me in that office, holding me as I navigated the darkest days of my life. She had been the unseen hand that guided my words and gave me the strength to honor my father.

Shortly after my father's passing, I felt a powerful call to visit Egypt. The call was undeniable, though I had never been and knew nothing about organizing a retreat there. Yet, as with all things guided by spirit, the path unfolded with ease. I was led to the right people, and together, we co-created a pilgrimage that was both a rite of passage and a remembrance.

We began in Aswan, the home of Isis, where I received her blessings. I swam in the sacred waters of her temple, allowing the Nile to cleanse and renew me, to dissolve all that stood in my way of fully embodying the divine feminine within.

Standing before the pyramids, I felt pure ascension light transmitting through my being, illuminating ancient codes that had long been dormant. It was a return to something I had always known, something etched into my very soul. In those moments, I received a message from her: "Sheherazad, you are a daughter of Atlantis, a priestess welcomed home and called to bring others here to receive their sacred activations."

But why me? Why was I chosen? The answers remained elusive—until my most recent retreat.

As we stood in the temple of the oracle in Siwa, our guide, Rabbie, recounted a cruel history. He spoke of Cambyses, the Persian warrior who punished the vanquished peoples there by ordering all worship of the deities to be banned, defacing the temples, and punishing those who resisted. A shiver ran through me. In that instant, I understood. I had led my group there, and she was giving me an opportunity to clear the karma of my ancestors, to restore what had been erased, to bring the sacred back into the light. The weight of this realization pressed against my heart, yet within it, I felt a profound sense of purpose. I was exactly where I was meant to be, stepping into a destiny that had been waiting for me all along.

Following my sacred activation, my connection to the goddess deepened with each passing day. I was guided to create goddess circles, spaces where women could gather to connect with the divine feminine. Each month, we honor a different goddess, and in their honor, I create ritual oils, ritual candles, and ritual teas infused with their essence. These circles have become sacred sanctuaries of healing and transformation. The goddesses whisper to me, urging me to go deeper. They insist that this work was not meant to be surface level. It is a call to full embodiment, a healing of the divine feminine within each of us.

This work is my life's mission. My relationship with Isis is one of deep reverence and remembrance. She came to me in my darkest hour, held me when I felt lost, and illuminated my path forward. She is the embodiment of divine wisdom, magic, and transformation, and through her, I have come to understand the sacred power of the divine feminine in all her facets. My devotion to her is a devotion to healing, to restoring what has been lost, and to rekindling the sacred fires within every woman so she, too, can remember her power.

This is my prayer: that every woman knows that she is not alone; she can lay her burdens at the feet of the goddess and find comfort in her embrace. Through this path, she can call all the fragmented parts of herself back home, step into her strength, and heal the deeply embedded priestess and witch wounds, knowing it is safe to emerge from the shadows once more.

The goddess energy is all around us, whispering in the winds, pulsing through the waters, calling us home. She is inviting us to rise, to spiral and dance in her sacred current, and to embody the divine feminine in its fullest expression once again.

I am forever a student of the goddess, a devoted priestess walking in her footsteps. I listen, I am led, and I am held. And when I surrender to her guidance, miracles unfold. My journey has been one of death and resurrection, of losing and finding myself over and over again.

I have devoted my life to prayer and service, to honoring the divine feminine and sharing her magic and medicine with all who are called. This is my soul's note—a song of devotion, a testament to the power of spirit, and an invitation to remember the divine within us all.

"This is my prayer: that every woman knows that she is not alone; she can lay her burdens at the feet of the goddess and find comfort in her embrace."

17

THE POWER OF PERCEPTION

Lilly Melgar

Perception. How extraordinarily powerful it is. How it redefines and completely transforms the way we see ourselves and the world around us. My journey has been long and, at times, excruciatingly painful, but it has led me to the most beautiful space: I am fully alive. I get to be authentically myself. And now, I bask in the warmth of living with joy as my natural state of being.

So what is perception? One may define it as a way of regarding, understanding, or interpreting something. Perception and belief are deeply intertwined. Together, they shape how we interpret our experiences, make decisions, and relate to the world and to ourselves. They form the unseen architecture of how we live.

Let's break this down:

1. **Subjectivity** ~ Beliefs and perceptions are internally constructed. They are not objective truths, but rather deeply personal interpretations of reality that are often shaped by our upbringing, trauma, and repetition. What we believe, we perceive. And what we perceive, we believe. That's why we often find ourselves living out the same situations repeatedly until we shift the lens through which we view them.

2. **They shape behavior** ~ Our thoughts and perceptions directly influence how we feel, respond, and behave. Just one limiting belief can distort our entire perception and hold us emotionally and mentally hostage for years, even decades. But when we begin to question those beliefs and rewrite the internal narrative, we begin to shift those mental patterns, and that opens the door to transformation.

3. **They build our mindset** ~ Together, beliefs and perceptions form the foundation of our mindset: the lens through which we see ourselves and our world. Change the lens, and the entire picture changes. That's not just spiritual wisdom; it's neuroscience and emotional alchemy.

Hi. I'm Lilly Melgar. I have had the privilege of enjoying some success as an actress, host, director, and producer. I've earned a couple of Emmys, loyal supporters, and some pretty cool credentials along the way. And yet, my most important and fulfilling gig has been that of being a mother to the most exceptional soul; my beautiful daughter, Sofia. My greatest teacher, soulmate, and healer.

Getting here wasn't easy. It took many deaths of different versions of myself. It took crawling out of crippling pits of grief. It took shedding layers of shame, regret, and self-judgment. It meant revisiting painful childhood events that not only impacted my psyche but also imprinted negative subconscious beliefs that would inevitably alter the course of my life.

Yet, here I am. Owning my essence unapologetically, knowing that every choice, every mistake, every heartbreak, every moment of despair, and all the loss was always leading me to a moment.

Can I honestly say I'm grateful for all the pain? I can't genuinely say that I'm there yet. I've barely embraced the stage of acceptance and made peace with it all. I'm still figuring it out as I continue to evolve.

One of the most pivotal shifts in my journey came through a conversation with a key mentor in my life, Oriah Mirza. As I sat across from her, drowning in self-judgment, sharing my story, the mistakes, the self-sabotage, the moments I felt I'd abandoned myself over and over again, she smiled.

She looked at me with a gleam in her eyes and said, "I love your soul! Your soul came to play full out in this lifetime! It came to experience the full range of the human experience! You're a badass!"

What?! Could I really see myself and my journey through that lens of possibility? It was more than a revelation; it was my liberation. In that moment, I exhaled with the deepest relief I had felt in years. To choose to see my journey through the lens of choice was invigorating! It shattered the victim mentality instantly. Look, the only person who will ever have to fully deal with you . . . is you. So why not choose belief systems that make being you the most empowering experience possible?

I began asking myself: "What am I choosing to believe right now?" That one question became a compass. I started a gratitude journal to help me focus on what was right in my world. I also journaled the story I had been telling myself and then rewrote a new one where I wasn't the girl who missed her shot, but the woman who reclaimed her power. This simple practice of observing my thoughts and choosing again became my daily alchemy.

We get to reframe our experiences to work for us instead of against us. We do this by choosing what we believe to be true. This isn't just our innate power; it's our magic. I need to share that I lived a solid decade of a charmed life. I was set up for big things, great things. My career options were endless. Life shimmered with promise and endless opportunities.

And yet, I made every choice that ensured I wouldn't reach the heights available to me at the time. Time and time again, I got scared, played small, shrank from the delicious goodness flowing in. I had no one to blame but myself. It was I who made those decisions. I, who didn't love myself enough to choose better.

And because of that, I carried an unbearable weight of regret, guilt, and shame. But with one sentence . . . one shift in perception . . . I was given the keys to my freedom. I get to choose what I believe to be true. I get to decide how I see my life, my choices, and my experiences.

As an actress, I've always known I can play life out in a multitude of ways. This life of mine is my movie; my reality. And now, I choose to believe that every twist, turn, and struggle was purposeful.

That I came into this lifetime to feel everything! The beauty, the pain, the exhilaration, and yes, even the loss. This is where focus comes in. I had to consciously focus on my journey not as one of victimhood, but one of victory. To see myself as the survivor that I am and embrace the self-respect that comes with owning that.

There was a time I saw myself as damaged goods because of everything I had endured, instead of seeing the extraordinarily resilient spirit that I truly am. A spirit who went through all of it and still chose to remain open to love, still chose to live fully, still believes in the good, and now owns her worth.

I had to learn to speak to myself differently. There were mornings I looked in the mirror and said through tears, "I love you, Lilly." I began whispering to myself, "You did the best you could." And over time, the whispers became a new inner voice rooted in grace.

Since Oriah, there have been many more women who've played key roles in my healing, growth, and rising. Women I refer to as soul sisters, not because of some trendy spiritual fad, but because these women have held space, been there, and loved me through all the seasons of my life.

My most recent mentor, Sheherazad Barnes, has been a mirror, a sacred space-holder, and a fierce advocate for my light, joy, beauty, and worth. She has called me to higher ground, gently, yet firmly. All while celebrating me with a love so pure, so unconditional, that I often find myself seeing glimpses of who I truly am through her eyes. She has led me to sacred lands for deeper understanding, soul remembrance, and ancestral healing. In her presence, I have felt both held and challenged in the most loving of ways. As a result, I finally felt safe enough again to embrace my Divine Feminine without fear. Without armor.

That alone is quite an accomplishment. I am forever grateful to her and all the other empowering souls (men included) who have held my hand, uplifted me, and loved me into this new version of self.

And in doing so, I have found my truth. Sometimes, we carry the weight of the past. Sometimes, we drown in self-judgment. I get that. But I also know the magic that lives in shifting our beliefs and perceptions. When challenges arise, as they always do, what if we asked ourselves: What if my soul chose this? What if my hardships aren't failures, but necessary steps towards awakening? What if I stopped seeing myself as broken... and started recognizing myself as whole, as powerful, as unapologetically me?

Because the truth is that we are. Whole and complete. And the moment we choose to see it, accept it, own it... that's the moment we set ourselves free. If you're in the dark right now, I want to offer a few tools that helped me reclaim my light:

- **Journaling:** Write your raw truth. Then write your reframe. Your pain is valid, but so is your power. I have constantly reinvented myself, and you can too.
- **Mirror Work:** Stand before your reflection and speak life into yourself. Even if your voice resists. Begin with a thought. Then try a whisper. Place your hand on your heart and begin to love yourself in the way you may have never been loved before.

- **Breath & Body:** Breathe deeply. Let your body feel safe. Movement and stillness equally matter. Mentorship: You don't have to do this alone. Find someone who sees you…who really sees you…and reminds you of your light when you forget.
- **Choice:** Ask yourself, "What would the highest version of me choose right now?" And then do that, even if just a little. One day at a time.

These are some tools to help us remember who we are. And I promise you, if I can get here, so can you.

18
LOVE + RELEASE

Tracey Rose

My obsession with the word 'release' was precipitated by a chance encounter. I was asked by a non-profit to host a concert for a Farm Trails Open House at an animal rescue site in Sonoma County. I was intrigued, available, and immediately on board. The setting was pastoral, the visitors energetic, and my interactions ranged from conversations with toddlers, parents, and grandparents to those with the band. As I stood off to the side of a dirt path that was used to access one portion of the property, a woman approached. She was wearing a canvas hat, a colorful flower print dress, and a welcoming smile.

"Hello," I said. "How are you doing?"

"I'm doing well. What an interesting day," she replied.

We formed an instantaneous bond and spoke in depth about the environment, the venue, politics, and our world. After a five-minute exchange, she asked if I could attend a "Release Party" she was hosting in June. I asked her what a "Release Party" was, and she answered: "Most people call it a 'Retirement Party,' but I call it a 'Release Party.'"

I said yes.

From that moment on, the word *Release* drew me in. It clattered around the sinewy landscape where muscle meets skin. It inhabited every cell, synapse, and tissue in my body. My dreams formed membranes, my waking life strung contextual connections like a mycelium network. Every relationship, situation, and opportunity was a portal to the word *Release*. The universe is the unspoken language of release: ebb and flow, inhalation and exhalation, holding onto and letting go.

I began looking back. The year 1972 was a transformational one for me. My marriage was in a state of 'dissolution' (the word they use in the divorce papers), I was back in school (after a two-year hiatus) in a new state, town, and college, with a new major (Theater Arts). Friendless, alone, broke. Housekeeping jobs, waitress jobs, and frugality were my lifeline. My options appeared bleak and precarious. I decided to finish my bachelor's degree and gird my loins for the future.

Enrolled at San Diego State University (SDSU) in Southern California, I dedicated myself to the unfamiliar curriculum of Theatre Arts, which included Play Analysis, Scene Design, Acting classes, Theatre History, Theatrical Makeup, and Directing. One of the early classes I took was Play Analysis, where the seating was in a circle. Sitting opposite me in class was a stunning blond, dressed in faded blue overalls, layer upon layer of estate-quality turquoise and silver jewelry, expensive shoes, flawless makeup. She exuded a kind of vivaciousness and luminosity I had never seen before.

I, on the other hand, was immersed in a profound state of depression—taking refuge behind an impenetrable barrier devoid of human connection. I was limping my way out of a fractured marriage, buried by a tsunami of guilt, sadness, and disorientation. My mental anguish was disguised as aloofness, sophistication, and mystery.

Janet, the stunning blond, was undaunted. She viewed me as her "God-given challenge" and forged ahead. We were polar opposites in character and disposition, but it did not deter her. It bolstered her resolve to rescue me from the abyss.

A voracious chain-smoker at the time, I spent my breaks between classes on the veranda, consuming as many cigarettes as I could manage in a ten-minute period. Avoiding interactions at all costs, I was hibernating in the open.

"Hi, I'm Janet. How are you doing?" was her audacious introduction.

Her smile landed like a thunderbolt in my ruptured ego, and she claims (though I don't remember saying it) that my response had been "Don't you ever NOT smile?"

Unphased by my cheek, she asked me what school I had transferred from (University of Washington) and told me about her move from Los Angeles to San Diego. In time, I embraced her relentless overtures to friendship and dubbed her "Sunshine."

I understood, almost immediately on a visceral level, that I had met my soulmate. I began wearing overalls, learned to laugh again, and nurtured a friendship that lasted beyond that veranda. This angel in human form became my best friend.

Janet's father had been a superior court judge when she was growing up. A product of the Great Depression, he knew the value of money only that generation could. He provided Janet with an allowance, but always insisted she work part-time to augment the money she received from him. While I was scrubbing toilets and ovens in wealthy San Diego homes, Janet was Xeroxing manuscripts, books, and other documents at one of the photocopy shops in town. Our depleted budgets left little room for frivolous purchases; nevertheless, Sunshine introduced me to Baskin-Robbins' gastronomic masterpiece: the Jamoca Almond Fudge milkshake. From that moment on, we were hooked.

We made a bi-monthly pilgrimage to the store as a reverent act of resilience in the face of poverty. It was a small victory that cost little more than one dollar and fifty cents, and the joy we shared was only comparable to the money we saved. It was our salvation in a world consumed by greed and power. We discussed upping our game at the semester's end and busting the bank with a banana split. Could we justify it, we asked? Expunge our indiscretion as a necessary reward for our backbreaking work and studious efforts? Collaboratively, we concluded it was.

Turns out, it was a billboard mirage full of hype, undeliverable in taste. Jamoca Almond Fudge regained its stature in the pantheon of flavors and reigned supreme until we graduated.

Sunshine was a musical theater actress; I was a dramatic actress. There was an unspoken chasm between the two: dramatic actors disregarded musical theater as "silly and playful. "Musical theater actors regarded dramatic actors as "arrogant and foolishly serious. "For that reason, she and I rarely competed for the same roles or were cast in the same productions.

Only once, in our first year, did we occupy the same stage. It was a children's show called "Aesop's Fallibles." The lead-in chorus began: "Rock, Rock, Rock with Old Aesop . . . we've rewritten all his fables!" My character was Amelia Eagle, and I strode on stage dressed as an Aviator Eagle with knee-high leather boots, a bomber jacket, goggles, and an aviator flapped cap. I don't remember Janet's character; I think it was a mouse. I do remember her on the other side of the stage, smiling at me between stage entrances. Her smile lit up rooms, and I was a benign recipient of her light. We toured a few elementary schools with the show before its run ended. It was our only ensemble work as classmates in the ensuing two years.

Janet was a constant fixture at an antique store up the street from her cottage. The "Prop Shop" carried every epoch of vintage framed prints, vases, bookcases, dishware, you name it. Her house was an eclectic display of exquisitely curated pieces. A natural interior designer, her well-appointed home was a haven for me. I was living in a small apartment when we met, with a foam pad for a bed, sleeping bags as blankets, and a small linoleum dining table furnished by the landlord. I had a sewing machine, which I used to make two oversized pillows, which became the only furniture in my barren living room.

My apartment didn't lend itself to entertaining, so we spent our weekends in her little house making and consuming chocolate mousse while engaged in prolonged metaphysical discourse. Topics included philosophy, religion, love, and the purpose of the arts in our lives. Though Sunshine came from a strict Presbyterian background, she was open to exploring divergent schools of thought. I, however, sensed a reluctance. When we strayed too far from the dogma of organized religion, there was noticeable discomfort. I, on the other hand, prayed to no god or altar. My mother had left the Catholic church, and with it, her faith. Zen Buddhism, Eastern Mysticism, Gurdjieff, and Krishnamurti had whetted my appetite for metaphysics. Knowledge, ideas, and words became my religion. I spent countless hours over endless cups of coffee discussing philosophy with PhD candidates in that field at the UW.

Time and circumstances had led me to re-examine my beliefs and values, as well as how I grappled with my catastrophic failure as a woman and a wife. Janet supported my investigations and introduced me to astonishing new-age writers and thinkers. Doors were opening. A burgeoning self-confidence was taking hold. Our love and friendship were deepening. Evolving. Flourishing.

The Butcher Shop restaurant in San Diego's Mission Valley was my waitress job two summers in a row while I was at SDSU. My tips and wages allowed me to live modestly and still have a meager savings for the following school year. Sunshine had suggested a trip to Maui, assuring me a relative could get us a deep discount on airlines and that we might be able to stay with my ex-brother-in-law.

I had never traveled much—except for a trip to Tijuana when I was married—and I needed a respite from waitressing, housekeeping jobs, and the numerous jobs I held on campus. We boarded the airplane with small bags, open hearts, and dreams of wild adventure in paradise. My brother-in-law picked us up and quickly arranged for us to stay with a friend who was a single dad with a thirteen-year-old son. His house was at the base of a small mountain with roads that were not easily navigable. Alan was hospitable, funny, and smart. As I recall, he was a geologist and worked long hours. We became babysitters for his son, Dewey, in his absence, and were given his extra car to explore the island on our own. Janet and I spent days at various beaches, movie days, a day at a Zen Buddhist center, island cafes, and galleries. They were endless days of no consequence, drifting aimlessly to whatever harmonic vibration beckoned us. It was a spiritual awakening for me, and a magnanimous gesture for Janet.

I fell in love and had an affair with my ex-husband's friend. I abandoned Janet to pursue this new love, and neither apologized nor reconciled that desertion of our friendship when we returned. Eventually, I saw that Janet's life had been a delicate balance of her rebellious spirit and her reckoning with patriarchal expectations. Worldly yet innocent, she taught me to live more freely. To love more freely. She had cracked my heart wide open, released my past and my pain, and let me go.

I graduated in 1974 with a BA in Theatre. Janet graduated three months later. I moved north and eventually remarried. She married and stayed behind, returning to Los Angeles to pursue acting jobs in Hollywood and live theater in rural settings. We were Maidens of Honor for one another's weddings, and she was with me when my water broke in a restroom at the bus station as I dropped her off for LA, and soon after, became the godmother to our firstborn. She was present for my children's graduations and accumulated anniversaries, for heartbreak and for triumph, for milestones and for setbacks. Janet was smart, kind, adventurous, crazy, beautiful, loyal, talented, generous, loving, and my friend. Unrelenting in her respect and love for me, she was a beacon of hope for the forty-six years we shared.

On January 3, 2018, a brain aneurysm took her within hours of her hospital arrival. Days passed as I came to accept that I was now the holder of memory for the two of us. How could I release her to the cosmos and know that our love had no end? That it was a "connecting thread that was unbreakable." That love is the language of the universe, and releasing our hold creates a space for it to inhabit.

"Sitting opposite me in class was a stunning blond, dressed in faded blue overalls, layer upon layer of estate-quality turquoise, silver jewelry, expensive shoes, flawless makeup."

19
ALL DADS MATTER

Ana Mercedes Rivera-Pagan

In 2002, I became Director of a social service agency in California's Central Valley. There had been three short-term directors in this agriculture-based county prior to my arrival, which was telling, but I took it in stride.

One particular day, I was staring at my list of things to tend to when I heard a soft knock on my office door. When I looked up, there was a young man standing uncomfortably in the doorway. He looked as if he contemplated running away.

"Director," he said. "Last week I attended your getting-to-know-you meeting. You invited us to speak with you directly if we had concerns or ideas to share. I looked for your secretary to make an appointment, but she wasn't at her desk. I hope you don't mind that I just knocked."

"Come in," I said, gesturing to a chair. I left my desk to sit across from him. I had only been on the job six months, and while remembering faces, I still struggled with names. "You look familiar. I think you were in last week's group. What's your name? What can I do for you?"

"My name is Cesar," he replied. "I'm in the eligibility department. I want to talk with you about the fatherhood program."

"Ahh, yes, The Fatherhood Coalition." I'd been to a couple of the meetings.

"Director, I heard you are considering cutting the program's funding. I came to see if you would reconsider."

"Tell me about your concerns," I replied. "Why should I reconsider?"

He replied, "I volunteer as a facilitator. I have two sons, and I had no idea what it meant to be a good father. My wife did everything for the children and the household. I went to work and came home so she could wait on me. I thought all I had to do was be a provider. I copied what my father did when I was a kid. I don't blame him; he worked hard in the fields, so he had nothing left to give when he got home. Through the program, I learned that being a dad was so much more, and that I needed to interact with my children."

"Who benefits from what you do with the program?" I asked.

He responded, "We have an annual contest in the schools where kids send in essays explaining why their father should be Father of the Year."

"Are there any other activities conducted throughout the year?"

"We have talks about what fathers should do."

"I see. Are the families these fathers belong to intact with both a mother and father?"

I knew for a fact that the larger percentage of households in our community were single-parent households of low income. In an agricultural community, they worked long hours in the fields or worked two jobs, with limited transportation. With few exceptions, most families in poor neighborhoods are headed by a single parent.

"Cesar, I have attended several meetings of the Fatherhood Coalition, and I cannot in good conscience continue to provide funds for the program."

"But Director, it's the only thing we have."

Cesar explained that he was the last standing facilitator and that the job was infringing on his family time. "I spend more time with other people's children and almost none with my sons," he said. "It's not fair to them."

I asked him to trust me, to let go of what existed. I promised him that I would work to develop a program that he would be proud of, one that he would be involved in planning, and that the new program would serve *all* men in the county. Two months later, the Fatherhood Coalition folded. After the political turmoil ended, I met with Cesar.

Although the door was open, he gently knocked. I waved for him to enter and take a seat. "I called for you because I made you a promise, and I intend to keep that promise. Are you ready to help with the new Fatherhood program?"

His eyes lit up, and the tired look on his face faded as he spoke. "I would love to help, Director, but I'm not certain how much time I would have to be of any help to you."

I laughed, "Let me worry about that. I am having you reassigned to a different unit. Today is Friday, and on Monday, when you come to work, you will report here. You are going to be part of my staff development team."

I had managed to create a new unit that would not only teach new employees how to do their jobs but also take on special projects. I reorganized existing teams so that both personnel and staff development reported directly to me.

"Cesar," I said, "You will work with me, and you are going to help me launch All Dads Matter. I understand that there is a Boot Camp for New Dads program that offers father-to-father, community-based workshops that equip men of different income levels, ages, and cultures to engage with their children, support their partners, and become more confident fathers. I want you to contact the developer and find out how we can obtain rights to the program he created. We are going to use this program as the foundation of our All Dads Matter project."

Cesar just stared at me with a look of wonder on his face.

"I also want you to find men like yourself who are passionate about being a father. I propose to open the All Dads Matter program to the entire community, inclusive of grandfathers, brothers, and men who fill the role of fathers."

Cesar sat quietly, stunned.

"Cesar, are you alright? Talk to me."

He fumbled his words. "I don't know what to say, except you are real. You kept your promise. I can't believe this is happening, but yes, it is. I want to work on All Dads Matter."

I smiled. "I'm glad you're on board. Just to be clear, your title doesn't change; you are still an eligibility worker at your current rate of compensation for a lot more work. However, I promise you that what you learn in staff development will prepare you for future advancement. Initially, you will be running the program by yourself. It will be some time before we can add additional staff. Cesar, I want to teach you how to hunt."

Startled, he said, "Hunt?"

"Yes, at some point, I want you to find at least five men of various ages who are as passionate about being fathers as you are. Ideally, this will be from within our staff because it makes it easier for me to move things around. However, an outsider can be considered as well. Hunt for talent and be prepared to tell me why you selected them for me to interview."

"Director, with all due respect," he began. "Why are you having me find people? Isn't that something that you do?"

I laughed. "Yes and no. Typically, recruitment is handled by the personnel department. But that's not what I want. I want you to find men who are passionate about being fathers. I don't know if you noticed, but I am not a man," I said.

Cesar grinned.

"My role is to design the program, find funding, teach you and the other facilitators what needs to be learned, ensure delivery, then step aside. The rest is up to you. Although," I added, "I will be monitoring success or hiccups. All Dads Matter *must* be about men helping men. No women will be involved except in support roles."

"But Director, won't the women be upset?"

I expected some frustration among the social workers, but I was prepared for it. "Cesar, do you tell your wife every detail of your day?"

"There are many things I will never share with my wife."

"And why is that?"

He cast his eyes down. "Because I don't want her to think of me as weak or ignorant."

I laughed and said, "Exactly. I rest my case."

"Director, one more thing. How does one hunt for talent?"

"Ahh, Cesar! First, you need to know what the ideal person looks like, so you build a profile. Once you know who you are looking for, you go to places where they live. You are looking for men who engage with their children and enjoy being fathers, so go where they take their children and observe how they interact. Get to know them if possible. Look for the yearning in people who want more and are passionate about doing something they love."

All Dads Matter was launched in 2003 with Cesar handling recruitment, facilitation, and coordination of all events. In 2005, we received a grant, and Cesar went hunting. Several weeks later, Cesar knocked on my door and said, "Director, I have some people for you to meet."

The first and most unforgettable was Lamar. He had a checkered history of employment but was working for a non-profit specializing in mental health issues and had earned a reputation for phenomenal engagement with clients. Energy exploded from every cell in his body. He spoke with passion and moved with excitement. During the interview, I learned that he was a parent of two girls, that he had been raised in Bakersfield, and spoke of his family with loving tenderness. Lamar won a position on the team in 2005. The other men Cesar selected for interviews were exceptional as well. He had become a hunter.

Having worked for an agribusiness agency early in my career, I was very familiar with the challenges and financial limitations of agricultural workers. Many households were single-parent families. Those that were intact were predominantly led by the mothers. In general, the father-child relationship was frail, a common generational pattern. Among the intact families, fathers often worked multiple jobs, but it was not enough for "extras" like recreation, excursions, or toys. Most of the men targeted for All Dads Matter would need help. It was clear that we needed to add a highly skilled social worker.

One day, I overheard a conversation between one of our social workers and our personnel manager. Richard was an excellent therapist who was also in the process of submitting his resignation. I walked into the personnel office, interrupting their conversation.

"Richard," I said. "Why are you leaving?"

"My father is ill," he replied, "And there is no one to help him. I asked my supervisor to adjust my schedule so I could take my father to his medical appointments. I offered to work weekends, but he declined. I have no choice. I must leave."

I turned to my personnel manager and confirmed that we had no policy to cover compassionate family leave. I turned to Richard. "Give me a week and you'll have a new schedule."

After the policy was in place, Richard came to thank us. Eventually, even though Richard retired before All Dads Matter was fully functional, he came back to work facilitating therapeutic sessions with the dads.

We expanded our services by partnering with other agencies. We offered conflict mediation training, job training, retraining and placement, parenting classes, and financial management. We taught them how to navigate institutions and advocate for themselves and their children. Whatever the need, we used our county resources to help men redefine themselves to become better fathers, better husbands, better sons, and more confident men.

The Family Resource Center, run by Dennis, provided parenting classes in multiple languages. The courts, law enforcement, and the community embraced the work of All Dads Matter. One of the elected officials on the Board of Supervisors sent his son to Boot Camp for New Dads. His son was so impressed that our client population grew across all cultures, economic levels, and ethnicities. An annual community event honoring fathers was held for community families. All Dads Matter gained state and national recognition for its groundbreaking work.

Fast forward to 2008, my team was invited to deliver a keynote address about All Dads Matter at a national conference. Cesar and Lamar were delighted but were adamant that the architect of the program should be the speaker. They were forceful in convincing the selection board that, without the leadership and warrior ability to make things happen, All Dads Matter would not exist. The committee relented and invited me to speak.

There were nearly 600 men in attendance and a scattering of women. Among them was Gladys Knight and her husband, a pastor passionate about fatherhood.

When the time came for me to take the stage, I began with the usual opening remarks, acknowledging the event organizers. After a brief introduction, I played a video we had created about the program, which featured staff, clients, and their children and spouses discussing the lessons learned and the value the program had added to their lives. A chorus of men shared how it had changed their lives. Children expressed gratitude for the fresh new connections they had with their fathers.

When the video portion of the presentation concluded, I took the microphone. "At the beginning," I began, "I promised to provide the background story of the program. Here it is.

The truth is, my dad was a person who had difficulty connecting with people. He was not one to show emotion. He didn't have many friends. The only men he hung out with were his brothers, and they were just like him. My father and I had a complex relationship. He favored me over my brother; perhaps it was because I was firstborn or maybe because I challenged him. He was not kind to my mother.

When Mom put his suitcase outside our apartment door, he left quietly. I did not see him often after his departure, but he did make a point of reaching out.

When I joined the army, I was trained as a medic and worked alongside the soldiers. I comforted men with lost legs, lost dreams, lost hopes, and listened to their cries late at night. In return, I was treated with respect and protected as a sister.

All Dads Matter is a program inspired by what I learned from my father and the wounded men I met along the way. I fought to bring life to the program so that children would have what I did not have. This program is a demonstration of love and forgiveness that I have for my father, Pablo Rivera-Martinez. He wasn't perfect, but he did the best he could. He was our Brooklyn neighborhood bookie—and I am the bookie's daughter."

20

FROM MEAGER MEANS TO BEING ALL THAT!

Viera Whye

"You have to keep on believin' and keep right on steppin'"

I grew up the youngest of thirteen children, six boys and seven girls. My family was of meager means (dare I say poor), and I had many wants that went unmet, but we always had everything we needed. I fondly remember my "village," a small black community of 30-40 families founded by ex-slaves. A place where everyone knew everyone. More than you may have wanted (there were always the nosy and gossipy neighbors). Everyone seemed to be an aunt, uncle, or cousin. I would later come to appreciate how safe, motivating, and instrumental this community would be in my life.

This place that I still call home (even though I moved away many years ago), "raised" their children and taught them respect, manners, discipline, commitment, and courage, which are all characteristics I carry with me through life. It was a place where folks cared for one another and demonstrated generosity and kindness. If there were a family in need of food, shelter, or financial support, someone would be there to help. If there was illness or death in a family, the community rallied around their neighbors to shoulder the pain and grief with prayer, plates of food, flowers, and open hearts. From this foundation, I would grow and learn professionally and personally.

I am of an age that I must mention racism, prejudice, and bias as part of my story. They were just facts of life that I would have to navigate. We lived surrounded by low to middle-class, to well-to-do whites. So being black and poor was an identity I was faced with as a child. I was the youngest "the baby" of my siblings, so I always felt special and loved. That love gave me the strength to hold my head high and to know my worth. I learned to see myself as "somebody" who was smart, attractive, vibrant, and capable. Realizing these qualities about myself would enable me to deal with adversity in a mature way and see beyond hatred and ignorance.

In High School, with several other students (one of whom was my niece), we began the Black Cultural Club (BCC), basically our Black Student Union (BSU). I was the President, and that role sparked my leadership journey.

I have also worked summer jobs since I was fourteen, doing clerical work at the YMCA and the Board of Education. I learned time management and attention to detail that would prepare me for project management roles later in life. I also worked in the principal's office after school. A lesson in humility and pride was learned through the job in the school office and as president of the BCC. Students seeing me in the office would know that my family needed money, and as president of the BCC, when the school delivered Christmas baskets to the needy in the community, my home was one of them, and it was I who was delivering the turkeys!

I remember being embarrassed initially, but I quickly overcame it and was confident and unapologetic about my economic status. I refused to let others' opinions diminish my respect for my parents and community. My Dad was a truck driver. He got up early every morning, went to work, worked hard, and provided for his family. My mother was a domestic and did what she needed to do to care for her family with dignity. I remember going to work with her to clean houses before I started kindergarten and having to enter through the back kitchen door.

Ironically, I was named after two of the ladies my mom worked for; fortunately, I love the name Viera. At times, I reflect on the fact that I've earned more money in a month than my dad made in a year, and today I hire house cleaners. Honestly, it seems surreal, but I honor them by remembering their sacrifices and acknowledging the blessings their foundation allowed me to build.

I find that the values I learned as a young girl continue to shape me. The poems, interpretive dance, and songs my mom and church elders would make me do at church and events (often unrehearsed and off-tune) prepared me for performing on stage. I gained confidence from the trust and belief these folks poured into me.

That confidence blossomed into advocacy. From elementary school on, I spoke up for classmates with disabilities, and later for those marginalized by race or other circumstances. I developed a passion for equity, inclusion, and justice—values that I would carry into my career. With a deep sense of empathy, I would find myself being a voice for others who needed a platform for their voices. I truly dislike bullying, selfishness, unfairness, classism, racism, sexism, and any other "isms." Folks need to treat others with compassion, understanding, and tolerance.

I feel it in my spirit to call out "ugliness and meanness." The sensibilities I had as a young girl have remained with me as I continue to be a voice for equity, equality, inclusion, and belonging across racial, ethnic, gender, and cultural identities. Through my work as a program, project, and people manager in high tech for more than 30 years, and diversity and inclusion specialist for the past 10 years for Tabia African American Theatre Ensemble (TABIA), and the artistic director for San Jose Multicultural Artists Guild (SJMAG) for 40 years, I have actioned my purpose to ensure folks know they matter and improve their wellbeing.

My passion and compassion for others and to always be true to myself ("to thine own self be true") and authenticity have led me to have a remarkable career in high tech, successfully lead a multicultural theatre company, and raise two incredible sons!

People often ask me how I do all that I do. And my answer is through the grace of God and determination, and to do it all with excellence. My mom used to say, "If you are not going to do it right, then don't do it at all."

Another motto that I also live by is "where there is a will, there is a way." Simply said, this is inspiration for me; perseverance has sustained me even when I wanted to give up. I rely on principles of strength and wisdom instilled in me by my mom and siblings to guide my work. I have been abundantly blessed, and it's important to me to be a blessing to others and to practice gratitude. One of my favorite gospel songs has the lyrics "If I can help somebody, then my living shall not be in vain." I hope to live my life in accordance with these lyrics.

SJMAG/Tabia are artistic companies that I have been a part of for 40+ years. Both share a mission to unite and serve communities by conducting cross-cultural arts programming reflective of the experiences of African Americans, women, and Latine. Under my leadership, we brought diverse cultural groups together to celebrate our similarities and differences; we staged programs that didn't shy away from meaningful social justice and topical issues; we provided quality, affordable, and professional theatre; and we worked diligently with youth, nurturing and mentoring their growth and development through the arts.

My inspiration and journey in theatre began as a teen after attending a Summer Acting Intensive. This lifelong experience as a performing artist continues because I feel deeply about people, peace, struggle, equality, tolerance, joy, love, despair, hopelessness, happiness, and unity. I need to express these emotions creatively to educate, entertain, and affect lives, and to challenge and embrace different beliefs. Theatre touches and stirs the soul . . . and in the words of Langston Hughes, "My soul runs deep like the rivers." Being the Artistic Director of Tabia has been challenging yet rewarding, competitive yet supportive, tiring yet energizing, and discouraging yet inspiring!

Beyond career and art, my proudest role is being a mother. I raised two amazing sons who embody strength, perseverance, determination, courage, and resilience. When one of my sons was in college and going through challenging times, I wrote this poem to encourage him and remind him of his courage and bravery in standing tall in the face of adversity.

Sometimes life is hard and Sometimes hard is life.
Sometimes it makes you want to holler, scream, cry, and shout.
But you have to keep on steppin'
Keep on walkin'
Keep on talkin'
Keep on smilin'
Keep on climbin'
Keep on movin'
Keep on lovin.'
Cause sometimes life is hard and Sometimes hard is life.
But—Such is Life.

Let no one, or anything hold you back.
Keep you down, make you wear a frown.
Keep you stressed, depressed, and in distress!
You have to keep on steppin'
Keep on reachin'
Keep on teachin'
Keep on preachin'
Keep on strivin'
Keep on thrivin'
And keep right on livin'

Your mind, and body, and soul, and spirit
Are yours to own, and value, and nourish, and treasure.
You just have to keep on dreamin', keep on believin',
  keep on prayin' and
Keep right on steppin'!

I am pleased to say my son worked through trying times and was amazingly successful. He overcame immense odds through determination, preparation, and undeniable talent. Both of my sons excelled as athletes from a young age. They played basketball, soccer, and football. Football would become their sport! They were extraordinary in high school and outstanding in college, earning scholarships after starting as "walk-ons."

Despite being unheralded in high school, unrecruited to college, and undrafted to the pros, both made it to the NFL and played significant time, an achievement that speaks volumes. Their physical, mental, and emotional ability to achieve the level of success to make it to "the league" was phenomenal. They overcame all odds to defy the systems, favoritism, and nepotism that are an integral part of the NFL and stand proudly as young men who made dreams come true. I supported and encouraged my sons to believe in themselves, trust their instincts, be wise in choosing their friends, be discerning with their time and money, and to be "good people." They did all these things and are marvelous men who lead vibrant and fulfilling lives.

I have been blessed with beautiful sister friends, loving brothers, and wonderful friends. When I moved to California from Baltimore many years ago, I knew only one person; today, I am connected to a vast community of colleagues and supporters. Throughout my journey, I have received numerous awards for my work in the arts, inclusion, and community service; however, the true rewards have always been connection, growth, and service to others. I am a member of several organizations that provide a platform to "give back."

This story serves as an example that you can achieve what you decide is best for you, regardless of circumstances and narratives others may script for you. You are bestowed with gifts that are yours to embrace and share with the world. My lesson was to learn that money and wealth can buy you comfort and luxury, but not happiness and joy. For me, happiness is found in good health, loving family and friends, and caring for others. True fulfillment is when I am present and "in flow." Peace of mind and being a good person are what truly nourish my soul and enable me to function at my highest potential. I got accustomed to being "the only" in many rooms and became an "overcomer." Since I was a kid, I have been able to let my light shine, continuing to thrive and inspire.

Looking back, I didn't just rise from humble beginnings; I rose with purpose. My story is not just mine; it's a tribute to my village, my parents, my sons, and to every dreamer who starts with little and dares to believe they can be "all that."

"I was the youngest "the baby" of my siblings, so I always felt special and loved. That love gave me the strength to hold my head high and to know my worth."

21
LOGGED IN AND CHECKED OUT

Ceara Fate

With the rise of the digital age, technology has been said to improve lives immeasurably. But as a Zillennial (too young to be accepted by Millennials and too old to relate to Generation Z) trudging through adulthood, I've found that social media and the internet have made connections more exhausting. There's a severe lack of depth in relationships. Humans weren't created to be available to the masses all the time. Our nervous systems weren't built to be connected to everyone we know with the click of a button. We've replaced face-to-face interaction with convenience. But is it easy on the body? The mind? Science says not really.

Though there are upsides to global connectivity, our bodies often feel otherwise. We feel empty when we don't get an instant response or when our messages are left unread without a response at all. We get dopamine hits from unexpected messages, especially the ones that start with "we need to talk." Many of us are unhealthily attached to the black mirror in our pockets, and we may feel close to others through real-time updates, but not in real life. Even those not chronically online struggle to find meaningful connections with others.

Instead of attending your cousin's birthday party 100 or more miles away, your family has a FaceTime gathering. Instead of getting the full college experience, you go to Zoom school and graduate through a glorified PowerPoint Presentation with a picture of you with an AI-generated cap and gown. Instead of attending community events, you attend TikTok livestreams and find internet friends you regularly converse with about your "real life" struggles through direct messages and video calls. What a wonderful digitally connected world we live in, right?

Growing up with the internet has been both a blessing and a curse. I first touched a keyboard at age three. My mom knew computers would be important and wanted me to start early. I got my first cell phone in fourth grade and a smartphone my freshman year of high school. My first social media account was a shared MySpace with my little brother at age eight, monitored by our mom. I learned to code glittery backgrounds and set my profile song to the current Fall Out Boy hit. Then came Facebook and Farmville. I created my own email when I was ten, made a Facebook profile solely to play games, and blocked my mom so she wouldn't see I existed on the platform—until she did. I also started chatting with strangers from my town, which could have ended badly if I hadn't learned internet safety from a young age. We were taught not to talk to strangers and to never meet up with people we really did not know in real life. This was deeply ingrained in us when we started using the internet around the MySpace era. Now I can spot a scammer every time they pop into my Instagram direct messages wanting to give me a psychic reading based on my profile picture and posts.

My parents sacrificed luxuries to send us to private school, which gave us an advantage when it came to using the latest technology. We took computer classes from kindergarten, starting with Microsoft Paint and CD-ROM games. By the second grade, we learned typing and basic Microsoft Office tools like Word, Excel, and PowerPoint.

By the fifth grade, we had to type the alphabet with our eyes closed. By the sixth, we were typing English essays and printing final drafts. I remember the relief of using backspace instead of rewriting everything by hand. But forgetting to save files to your USB drive (and not the library computer) meant losing all your work. Thankfully, most of us had home computers by then and could save our work there safely.

By high school, all essays had to be typed and formatted in MLA or APA style. We submitted to TurnItIn.com to check for plagiarism. Teachers docked points for font size and margin errors, even pulling out rulers to check. After I graduated, new students were issued laptops instead of textbooks. But in college, most professors still required printed textbooks, but PDF versions found on Google or by older students were shared without the professors' knowledge to save money. Often, we didn't even need them at all. Professors relied on slides or emailed free materials because they knew how ridiculous textbook costs were, and the school forced them to require a textbook. We learned to wait until week one before buying anything.

The internet does make life easier. But it has made me feel less capable. How is a kinesthetic learner supposed to retain information through an LED screen? When classes went remote in the final stretch of my senior year of college in 2020, I retained nothing. It was too easy to goof off—minimize Zoom, scroll Instagram, or play games. Professors gave pity A's because they didn't know how to teach online. I was admitted to a Master's program during lockdown, dreaming of moving to Los Angeles to pursue a career in the music industry. But the university announced the entire program would go remote shortly after the first semester had concluded. I was crushed. My plan was shattered. But there was no turning back as I had already taken out a pretty penny in student loans.

On the one hand, tech lets us reconnect with old friends. Classmates from kindergarten show up under "People You May Know." Someone you just walked past in the grocery store requested to follow you because you were recommended to them, and you had a familiar, friendly smile, and apparently a recognizable face. Your parents are able to keep in touch with family on the other side of the world. A random European man offers friendship and cash, which is clearly a scam, but your grandmother thinks he is truthful and REALLY loves her. They know you, or think they do, based on your profile. But do they?

It's very clear to me that parasocialism has replaced deep, meaningful relationships. Parasocial relationships form with celebrities, influencers, or anyone with an online platform. We feel like we know them—their routines, opinions, moods. But we don't. And often, we barely know our loved ones. Parasocial relationships are one-sided relationships that individuals often form with public figures, celebrities, and influencers, where they invest emotional energy into the relationship, while the public figure is completely unaware of their existence. It is like when your friend claims they are friends with Kylie Jenner because they sent her 50 Instagram DMs that were not even opened. It makes me feel queasy that there may be people on the internet out there who think they are close with me, but it is just a parasocial connection that I know nothing about. There are many lurkers on the internet who are getting to know you by your posts without conversing with you at all. Why visit a friend when you can watch their story unfold in real time? You don't need to be famous to share the glamour of everyday life.

No one knows that your profile is just a highlight reel. No one knows that you are really aching for someone to show up and give you a hug, unwarranted, because you have been feeling less than enough. No one knows that your grandmother has been battling stage IV cancer, and you're her main caretaker. No one knows you have bounced from therapist to therapist just to feel an ounce of happiness. No one knows. All they know are the aesthetically curated meal photos, the videos of the rowdy concerts you attend, the nature pictures with cryptic captions, and the impromptu selfies with enough editing to hide your insecurities. Everything is a curated experience. However, the 'experience' is really just your perception. We want to be perceived as a polished version of ourselves, or even someone else entirely.

Finding people you resonate with deeply feels like finding a goldmine in Antarctica. Who wants to sit with your shadow when it's easier to download an app to meet new friends in your area and move on to someone new? True care shows when people stick through the hard stuff. But now, it's easier to curate than to connect. Where has all the love gone? Into the ego. Into the persona we perform, not the one we embody when no one's watching.

The pressure to be prim, proper, and aesthetically pleasing is suffocating, thanks to influencers and the media shaming those who aren't perfect on a daily basis. But none of us is perfect. That's the beauty of being a spiritual being inhabiting a human vessel.

Even though I still fall victim to being chronically online, I'm reclaiming time in the physical world. I'm human. I'm aging. I want to live more under the sun, not behind a screen. I want to find people who will put down their phones and ask how I really am, and actually care. We're lucky to be here on this planet together. The internet could disappear in an instant. But we will always have each other. We can't take our physical nature for granted.

I hope the next generation, raised with iPads in hand, learns that too. It's our duty to remember that being human isn't the problem. Wanting to escape it is.

"Growing up with the internet has been both a blessing and a curse. I first touched a keyboard at age three. My mom knew computers would be important and wanted me to start early."

22

A LEGACY OF SERVICE

Leonard Weingarten

Having crafted a marketing career in civic engagement that has spanned decades, I've come to realize that true leadership doesn't always make headlines—it shows up early, stays late, and often stands just outside the spotlight. I cut my career teeth in organizing large-scale activities straight out of college, and I feel very strongly that service-driven leadership has been at the heart of what I do. For me, leadership is about service, not status.

I think one thing that attracts me to my work is helping to motivate and encourage people to raise their expectations of themselves and what they are capable of. You can do that either by being in front, or you can do it from behind, or next to them. I've been involved with very high-visibility enterprises. I've always been attracted to large-scale projects with great impact.

Lifelong learning has also been a focal point for my work. In the early 1990s, I was invited by the University of California, Berkeley, to teach a marketing course. I designed a sports events management course, which I taught for five years to an international audience. The curriculum covered large-scale event management and all the steps involved in achieving successful outcomes, from concept to conclusion. The culture at Berkeley is very diverse; it was like having a mini-United Nations in my classroom, which was great, and I loved it. I also learned a lot because sometimes you get in the habit of using "insider" jargon particular to an industry, and people don't know what you're talking about, so you have to thoughtfully deconstruct the jargon to reach your audience.

I brought in industry leaders as guest speakers and arranged industry field trips to reinforce the classroom discussions. As a class, we attended the World Figure Skating Championships and a soccer match between the United States and the Soviet Union national teams.

Once we arrived at the venues for the events, I told my students, "Keep your eyes open and notice how things are handled." This included the logistics, the layout, all the details, everything.

Normally, when people go to an event, whether it's a concert or a sports event, their biggest concerns are "Where do we park?" and "Where are our seats?" They have no idea of the months and years of preparation that go on behind the scenes to make a concert or an international sporting event happen.

Learning experiences don't always turn out like you think they might. For the US-USSR soccer match, we met with the event organizers, who gave us a tour of the stadium. After the soccer match, one of the students said to me, "Mr. Weingarten, I didn't realize how much work it is to put on these types of activities. I hope you don't mind, but I don't think this is right for me."

I wasn't upset. I told her, "If this type of work isn't for you, go find your passion. I don't take it personally."

I also spent a couple of years fundraising with the United Way of the San Francisco Bay Area, which is a large fundraising operation. At that time, the San Francisco United Way was the number five organization in the country, size-wise, and I had success across industry lines throughout several counties, including San Francisco, raising record levels of financial support for humanitarian services.

I have always tried to put a great focus on customer service and matching needs to resources. Enterprise for High School Students was a San Francisco city-wide agency that trained and provided students with a positive introduction to the work world. Based on a study conducted by Enterprise in collaboration with Harvard Business School, a position was created, and I was hired to develop and spearhead their relationships with the corporate sector.

On day one, I go to my desk and there is a piece of paper. That was my department. Three years later, Enterprise for High School Students was recognized by the US Department of Labor as one of the leading youth development nonprofits in the country. I was there for six years and loved it. Every professional has had a first job. It was very relatable and easy to build mutually beneficial bridges.

I reached out and partnered with people from the San Francisco Chamber of Commerce, Charles Schwab, Bank of America, and other leading local to national businesses. I asked my contacts, "How did you get started in your career?" It's an easy ice breaker and one that people are eager to talk about. As a result of my outreach efforts, I was able to organize job shadow days with Merrill Lynch, the San Francisco Giants, banks, and other worthwhile ventures for the students.

As part of the scope of the project, I expanded Enterprise's summer gardening program to the Golden Gate National Park Conservancy. This job training program saved the city more than $2 million because the students had on-the-job training in environmental studies and horticulture. I also appeared on numerous radio shows and other media outlets to spread the word.

There is a lot of passion in what I do because my motivation is always for the greater good. I'm always looking for the "why" behind the "what." I always ask myself, "Is this for the greater good? Am I learning something new?" I try to learn something from everyone, because everyone has a story and something to share.

Even though I've worked for large and impactful enterprises, I'm entrepreneurial at my core. I'm a risk-taker and I've been called persistent, which are very entrepreneurial assets.

For example, when I lived in Los Angeles, I saw an ad in the newspaper for an international sports conference that was coming to town. I couldn't afford the registration fee, and I really wanted to attend. Back then, we didn't have computers like we have today. I picked up the phone, called the number in the ad, and it went to the organizing office in New York City. I was put in touch with the President.

Remember, this was a cold call. We talked and worked out an agreement. In the end, she said, "Leonard, you help me with logistics and be my event manager; you get in for free."

So there I was, with world leaders in the sports industry, including England, France, Japan, China, Denmark, and the United States. I think I like high-visibility events because it is an opportunity to have a tremendous impact on many people's lives and to be part of something bigger than myself.

When I lived in Los Angeles, I enrolled in a sports communication program at USC. Even though I had industry experience, I wanted to meet people that the broad scope of USC contacts offered. While there, I applied for and was brought aboard to coordinate the publicity for the Official 1984 Los Angeles Olympic Games Retrospective Exhibit. This was a collaboration between the City of Los Angeles, the Los Angeles Olympic Committee, and the Natural History Museum of Los Angeles.

The museum didn't have a budget for public relations, which was great for me as I loved the entrepreneurial challenge. In the end, we reached more than three million people.

I partnered with Olympic athletes and had my stories featured on National Public Radio. It was heartbreaking when the exhibit closed because it was phenomenal. The collective impact of the exhibit extended beyond the L.A. Games. It also covered the history of the entire Summer Olympic movement, dating back to its inception in 1896.

Once the Olympic exhibit was over, I had the opportunity to work for a national public relations firm that handled the Rose Bowl Parade and Game. Following the game, I ran into a colleague from the public relations firm whom I hadn't seen in a while. A few weeks later, he called me and said, "Leonard, do you have any plans in the near future?"

Always open to opportunities, I replied, "Why do you ask?"

"The Pope is coming to the United States, and the local organizing company needs some help. Are you available?"

The Pope?! I replied in the affirmative, and he continued, "Good, because I've already given them your name and they're expecting you."

Pope John Paul II visited Los Angeles in September 1987, and he attracted a massive international audience. I was brought on board as one of the production coordinators for a two-hour Hollywood show preceding the Pope's Mass at Dodger Stadium, which served as the host venue. I worked with 1,200 international entertainers and many Hollywood personalities. I like to say that when my friend Peter reached out to me about helping the Pope, I received a 'calling.'

I'm very fortunate as I'm able to work effectively with everyone from volunteers to personalities to civic and business leaders. It's a broad spectrum. As an organizer, you need to be able to look at the big picture and also figure out the steps needed to make it happen, while keeping all stakeholders in the loop.

I continue to do a lot of volunteer work. In part, it's about giving back. It's sharing what you have and also a bit of personal growth. I never want to stop learning. If I see opportunities to be a resource for others and if I can help them, I want to do it. If I can help steer people in a direction that enriches their lives, why wouldn't I?

That is what leadership means to me: leading by example. The measure of a person is not so much what they say, but what they do. I try to be supportive of others. I endeavor to be thoughtful, considerate, and to see things from other people's perspectives.

My volunteering started as a teenager. I volunteered for KQED, the local public television station, working the phones when they had fundraising auctions. While in college at California State University, Chico, I was a Big Brother. I also had my own radio show, a sports show, of course. It was great because at that time I worked for the Oakland Raiders. I had access to the players, and during the summer training camp, I could interview the players. I could play those interviews throughout the fall. No one else at the radio station had that kind of access, so I had a unique niche.

Having enjoyed a career spanning fifty years, my greatest ambition continues to be building community. I want to be active and involved. I believe I still have a lot to offer, and as the CEO of the advertising firm Chiat Day once said, "You don't ever want to reach a peak, because once you peak, you're going down the other side."

We all have the opportunity to be part of a larger movement, and our participation makes our community stronger. When we are active, we appreciate one another, we build opportunities for people to become engaged, and we learn and grow. From this place, we can appreciate the cultural differences and the diversity of our community. If I can play a role that advances the sense of community, I'm in.

It's all part of lifelong learning, and if I can create relationships that benefit all parties, we all benefit. I've lived in Marin County for more than 30 years. I met my wife on Christmas Day, 1991, and once we married, we made Marin our home. This is where we raised a family and where we both continue to be part of the fabric of this community.

I would like to be remembered as someone who gave his best and wanted to make a positive impact on people's lives. I want to continue growing and challenging myself, being a positive role model for others, and being a vital member of the community.

I'm a collector of inspirational quotes by various leaders. One that sums up my devotion to community building is, "If you cannot risk, you cannot grow. If you cannot grow, you cannot be your best. If you cannot be your best, you cannot be happy. If you cannot be happy, what else matters?"

I've been fortunate in my life opportunities. I try to push myself, to learn something, and to make a positive difference. I would like to be remembered for my contributions.

*"If you cannot risk, you cannot grow.
If you cannot grow, you cannot be your best.
If you cannot be your best, you cannot be happy.
If you cannot be happy, what else matters?"*

23

CULTIVATING COMPASSION

Ken Harootunian

I've worked in the public sector for almost my entire career. I have had the great good fortune to have worked with both large institutions and smaller community organizations to support philanthropy and contribute to the public good. As I look back at my life, I've come to this work of intentionally trying to support humanity by closely watching and drawing inspiration from my father; after all, what child does not observe everything a parent does? My life has been enriched by my father's entire history, where he engaged as an active, average citizen of New York City, serving in WWII, and also by the values he so admired in the Armenian community.

My grandfather was born in Yerevan, Armenia, the capital of Armenia. As a young adult, he and his family, like many others, fled elsewhere once the Turks came through Armenia to wipe out the population. They went to Romania first, and then migrated to New York in 1905 and settled into a growing Armenian American community there.

At that time, as an ambitious young man, my grandfather worked as a porter for an Armenian rug dealer and learned the trade. He learned English as well, and within about five years, he went out on his own. Without any inventory or any assets, he started cleaning rugs for people, and oftentimes he would take rugs in trade for cleaning. He built up his inventory slowly, but ultimately, by the 1930s, he was paying someone to go overseas and purchase handmade rugs directly from various countries.

After both my father and my uncle served in World War II, my father went to Columbia University in New York, and my uncle went to NYU School of Engineering. Because my father was an art history major at Columbia, he had a historic and aesthetic affinity for the business, so it was natural that he joined it right after college. My uncle probably would have preferred a career in engineering, but felt an obligation to the family business, especially when my grandfather fell ill and passed away in the 1950s.

My father was passionate about the business, and he had a companion there in my uncle. My father was an extrovert, so he was usually the one to engage customers who came in off the street. They both went on house calls and to auctions, both in New York and in Philadelphia, for many decades, as they both knew the business and the opportunities to acquire antique rugs for their inventory. But my father's passion for the business was clear.

By 1990, even though I was a fairly advanced nonprofit professional, it became clear that it was now my turn to support the family business, even though I was not asked by anyone in the family. My uncle was recovering from a heart attack, and my dad was solo, hoisting heavy rugs by himself in his 60s. That was not a formula for success, for either the business or his long-term health, so I agreed to put my nonprofit career on hold for five years. The goal was to liquidate everything within that time so both my uncle and my father could retire, and I could move to California. I made the choice for family, no regrets. Sometimes your life takes a detour, right? I even learned a bit about woven arts, geography, the Silk Road, and history, even though rugs themselves were not my passion. I also gained a greater perspective and appreciation of my uncle's outlook on the business, as someone who was not as passionate about the art and industry as my father but felt an obligation to family.

During those five years, we sold most of the rugs through Sotheby's and Christie's in New York, and also a then small and new auction house in Boston called Grogan and Company, which took many more rugs than the two NYC auction houses combined. Five years later, in January of 1995, the showroom was cleared of the 1,100 often antique and always hand-knotted rugs that had occupied the cavernous space. It was then that my father was able to retire and "go play with the flowers in his garden, as he had played with the textile flower art in the rugs" for over four decades.

From a young age, maybe five or six, I used to go to work on Saturdays with Dad (it gave my mom a break from dealing with me and gave my dad and me that important bonding time). Six days a week, he would commute from the suburbs in northern New Jersey to Manhattan, and he would always say hello to the George Washington Bridge toll takers, and he never failed to say, "Thank you" when he got the change back from them, even though they would almost never greet him back (or say anything most days).

One day, I finally asked, "Why do you always do that? They never say, 'Hello' or 'Good morning' back to you."

My father paused and answered, "Ken, think about their job. They're sitting there in a booth year-round, with really cold weather in the winter, and really hot weather in the summer, no heat, no air conditioning. They're breathing automobile fumes. They have a hard life."

In today's world, we would call that compassion or empathy. Until then, I didn't see people as he did, as I was just a kid. But I was learning to be polite: Saying hello back to people who said hello and saying thank you and please, as my parents taught me. My father grew up in New York City in the 1930s-50s, learned to survive and thrive in the seven million or so people who inhabited the City during that time, and also served in close quarters with other young men from all over the country on a small destroyer ship in the U.S. Navy in the Pacific during WWII.

In that lesson at the George Washington Bridge that day, he taught me to see people in their adversity while maintaining a level of civility and polite discourse. My dad always talked about civil society up to the point when he passed at 96 a few years ago. Maybe that's why I'm drawn to those values.

I was raised to be polite. This means thanking people. It means saying please. It's following up in a timely manner. It's actually doing what you tell people you plan to do. It's thinking of people and their interests and how to keep them updated and informed about the things that we're mutually passionate about in the work or activities that we represent. It all seems very natural to me, but I know a lot of people were not raised to be polite; you don't hear thank you, see a gesture of gratitude, or even an acknowledgment sometimes. As far as I can remember, my mother never let me out of the house unless I was polite, and as I later learned, the parents in our neighborhood compared notes about how well (or poorly) behaved the neighborhood kids were.

The golden rule is a standard in just about every organized religion. And, it makes a lot of sense. It keeps us from escalating disagreements and killing each other, and even encourages us to keep cheering each other on. It's survivalism. It's total pragmatism. This is the backdrop of my father being raised as a first-generation Armenian American in New York.

In a City of now eight million people, you learn to survive. You learn to avoid confrontation in the streets, especially when you don't make eye contact. In my 20s, I used to revel in taking the bus every day from New Jersey to Port Authority, walking from Midtown on the West Side to 75th and Fifth, which is a very long walk. And I used to love making eye contact because it was daytime. I didn't fear anything or anyone and would just look into people's eyes if they would allow it. Most people keep to themselves and avoid eye contact in New York, as you may have experienced. It can be overwhelming and sometimes even dangerous.

When you look into someone's eyes, you look into their lives to some degree. Of course, what they're thinking and what you're thinking are rarely the same thing. I think the reason that people do not say hello is that there are just too many people to connect with. If you do take that leap of saying hello on the street in New York, it's a very quick thing, but those impressions make you realize how significant humanity is when you're amongst that many people, especially if a smile comes with it from the other person. I think you have to learn how to survive in that world, but also be a good citizen within it.

And that's where the concept of civil society is important. This was not something my father prescribed. It's just something he lived.

On the darker side, I think most New Yorkers are prepared for the worst, which is why they're able to cope with things when they do go south. And you know, this is not to deny a history of bad things happening; the worst (a genocide) has happened in my Armenian culture, as it has in some other cultures and religions. As a result, we learn to be prepared. It doesn't mean that we're able to deal with it in the moment when something happens, but by preparing for the worst-case scenario, you are not surprised, and you are at least somewhat ready.

The last century's Armenian genocide impacted my father because it directly impacted his parents, aunts, uncles, and grandparents.

Those who survived came to the new world, often settling in NYC in a growing Armenian American community that took care of each other, much as my grandfather was taken in by an Armenian rug dealer when he arrived in 1905.

The PTSD and generational trauma were pretty significant for my grandparents. They made it to the new world, but so many relatives and friends did not. My father, his brother, and his sister all heard the stories of the sadness and the loss. They all also went to college, and they created lives for themselves and our extended families. Being the first generation to go to college is difficult, as you have no family members who can help you. Having worked for two universities in my career, I see that kind of determination as heroic. Securing sponsorship funding so that first-generation college students could attend those schools resonated deeply with me when I worked at those schools.

And so I now bring all of this history and these considerations to my work as a nonprofit leader because so many plans can go awry. You have to think about all the interested parties (including clients, donors, staff, and board members) and never forget to leave any of them out, so each one of them feels like they're being treated with respect and like they were part of the solution or success, because they typically were in one way or another. They are all VIPs and should be treated that way whenever possible.

Ultimately, my father taught me about relationship building without ever discussing it. Absolutely everything in life is about relationship-building. Selling rugs is about relationship building. Matching funders to noteworthy nonprofits is about relationship building. And that's something that I experienced watching him work (with decorators, designers, architects, and their clients), both of us as adults, in those final five years of the family's rug business in the early 1990s.

As an example, in the late 1980s, my father and uncle's business was on the ground floor at 54th and Madison, a very busy retail part of Manhattan. The ground-floor showroom of the building that they were renting was sold to CVS. As a condition of honoring the lease, the new buyer relocated our family business to a sixth-floor showroom that was in the Decorators and Designers' Building at 62nd and First. Those relationships with the decorators, designers, and architects, the people who were the conduits to new clients, became very important as people could not just come into a street-level store anymore when you are on the sixth floor.

Thanks to my father, I can listen, ask follow-up questions, and try to put myself in other people's shoes, understanding where they're coming from. This is not just for work. This is just life. Because of my father, I developed this ability to listen deeply.

As a natural extrovert, I'm equally okay being quiet and observing. It allows me to quickly gain a sense of what I want to take away from most conversations. I ask myself, 'Does it build compassion? Does it build empathy?' You can't fake those things. You have to have a genuine interest in people, their stories, and their backgrounds.

In my work now in Sonoma County, we have a nonpublic high school called Journey Academy. In this remarkable place, we give kids without a lot of educational options the chance to change the narrative of their life stories. They come in thinking and being told that they are "bad students." and we show them all the good things they do, every day, and it flips the script by putting them on a path of positivity and forward-thinking about what they can do and accomplish in the world.

What happens when you change the narrative? You begin using a new language to frame your story. That's an amazing gift because when you tell and feel a different story about yourself, you have the chance to become a better version of yourself, as you define yourself, not as society defines you.

We all have the opportunity to leave a lasting legacy. My grandfather's legacy was coming to this country, cultivating community and opportunity, and raising a family. My father found meaning in his life by trading in beautiful and historic things and cultivating empathy and compassion for everyone he encountered. I loved and admired him for that.

When all is said and done, if someone were to ask me, I think I'd like my legacy to be kindness... kindness and perhaps storytelling.

24
RIDING THE DRAGON

Yukiko Amaya

Up in the rocky hills surrounded by the most ancient forest in France, I am sliding down deeper into a dark cave. The ground is steep, uneven, and muddy; the walls are wet. The ceiling of the cave disappears into a pointed and narrowing darkness way above me. The cave narrows in, and I am hearing a voice beckoning me to come in deeper. I see deeply recessed into the end of the cave, in the dancing light of a few votive candles, an alcove where there are small offerings left by previous pilgrims. Flowers and small crystals flicker in the uncertain light. Rising above that natural altar is a moving, shifting image of the dark goddess, dancing amongst the stone folds of the cave. I sink to my knees.

I should know, after years of practice and meditation, leading and performing ceremonies to the Great Mother for the benefit of all, that said Great Mother can knock you over in the name of awakening at any time. She will do it in any way She sees fit for your particular soul and human contours that are in resistance, and yell *loudly* in your ear ...Wake Up!

Rewind about 10 months back from the cave...I was decorating our beautiful Christmas tree, thinking about the busy, wonderous, and challenging year 2023 had been. After the isolating years of COVID, I had successfully resurrected the Earth Goddess Sacred Immersion journeys I design and lead for women to sacred sites around the world. In the fall of 2023, we went into Wales, the magical land of dragons and faeries, Goddesses and myths, high mountain lakes and craggy coastline bordering the wild sea. I had been prepping the Wales journey for a couple of years when COVID shut down the world as we knew it. It was the right moment to go back and be guided by the goddesses Cerridwen in the North and Rhiannon in the South. Cerridwen with Her cauldron of magic and regeneration and poetry, and Rhiannon, the goddess of sovereignty and horses and wild feminine. The Divine Feminine rises and sings powerfully through Land, Sea, and Sky in Wales.

In early 2023, I started promoting this mystical journey into Wales and, at the same time, began studying with the head Druid of the Anglesey Order of Druids and devotee of Cerridwen, Kristoffer Hughes, to prepare myself. It was a huge amount of work, and as usual, the rewards were incomparable. The most beautiful and diverse group of women came together. It was a powerful adventure and journey into Wales, as well as a deep dive into the magical wilderness within ourselves.

After completing the Sacred Immersion and saying farewell to the Wales group in London, I traveled to the foothills of the Pyrenees in France on my own, guided by the voice and presence of Mary Magdalene. I spent two weeks there, and powerful, miraculous things happened. At one point, I was led into the center of a field at Montsegur, where there had been a huge massacre of the Cathars on March 16, 1244.

The Cathars were a Christian sect that emerged mysteriously in southern France and northern Italy in the 12th century, treating both men and women equally. Some say they carried on the original teachings of Love of Yeshua and Mary Magdalene. They were deemed a heretical sect by the Catholic Church, and a crusade was waged against them until Catharism was totally eradicated. I was afraid to step into that field, where so many men, women, and children had been burned alive.

But when I followed Her voice into the heart of the flame, all I felt was an immense sense of peace. "Path of Love" was all She kept murmuring to me that day as I made the steep ascent to the ruins of Montsegur castle at the top of a towering, clifflike peak. I had a sense that I was being led onto a new path of teaching and initiation, but I was unsure as to what that was exactly.

As if to underline this new Path of Love direction She was leading me onto, I got married a month after I returned from the soul-bursting journey with Goddess. My beloved Skipper and I had already planned to get married on our land, a sacred space in the Blue Ridge Mountains, before I left. It was a powerful and beautiful pagan ceremony filled with connection to all beings, overflowing with love, surrounded by family and friends. The November day was sparkling, warm with the bluest sky and all the leaves in the forest in glorious golds and reds.

I felt so blessed after such an epic year. Yet, as the Winter Solstice of 2023 started to roll around, my inner life began to unravel. I would get irritated at little things like a cat being rubbed the wrong way. And then, my husband's back, which had been getting worse, went out altogether. He literally could not move without enormous pain and was spending most days and nights lying flat on the floor. The care of the house, of our animals, shopping, cooking, all fell upon me. I was really worried about Skipper's health. Christmas was fast approaching. I was also doing a full load of my own work as a healer and priestess.

A couple of days before the Winter Solstice, when I was finally able to get to the burned-out lightbulb in the kitchen ceiling, I was in a right cranky mood. This was not unlike when I was a teenager, still living at home, and feeling as if I were being contained in a too-small cage.

To reach the ceiling lightbulb, I climbed up on top of the kitchen counter. *Maybe you should go get the ladder?* An internal voice whispered, which I mentally swatted aside like an annoying fly. *I've done it this way before,* I muttered under my breath, *and I have so many things I need to get done, I can't be bothered to go fetch the ladder out of the garage.*

My body tense, my mind on the next gazillion things that needed to be tended to, I stood on top of the counter and simply stretched both my hands out towards the dead light bulb recessed into the ceiling.

When my body started to topple over in slow motion, I was so surprised I didn't grasp what was happening right away. I had leaned out too far forward, and now my body was falling towards the kitchen island. With horror, a thought flashed through my mind that this might be how I die. Broken neck, head, or back seemed to be the choices. My life energy drew in tightly as I closed my eyes. The next moment, I struck the floor, but miracle of all miracles, my body had somehow twisted sideways, and my head, neck, and back were all intact. I had missed the kitchen island. Then the blinding pain hit. It was my left heel. An awful howl and scream uncoiled out of my body as I started to convulse in pain.

The diagnosis was a smashed heel bone. No surgery, thank goodness, but no putting any weight or pressure on it for three months. This somewhat plebian, accidental fall in the kitchen is how my descent into the Underworld began.

In the "Descent of Inanna," a poem written by the Sumerians around 3000 BC, we are told that Inanna, the Queen of Heaven and Earth, *"opened her ear to the Great Below."* The word "ear" in Sumerian is the same as their word for wisdom. Something beyond conscious understanding and of a higher power is calling Inanna to pay attention, and She decides to *"abandon heaven and earth to descend to the underworld."* There, she must go through seven gates, and by order of Ereshkigal,

Inanna's sister and Queen of the Underworld, at each gate, she is stripped of an item of her power.

The first to go is her crown, then her lapis beads at her throat, then her long double-strand lapis necklace, then her golden breastplate, her golden bracelet, her lapis measuring rod and line, and finally, her royal robe. She enters the Underworld completely naked and is struck down dead by the look of death in Ereshkigal's eyes. She is put up on a meat hook and hangs there for three nights.

My own descent is taking a long time. At the time of this writing, it has been well over a year since my boot came off, and I started taking the first painful, tentative, and tottering steps towards re-educating myself to walk. I had grand plans when I was told I could not walk for three months. I decided to sign up for a ten-month course on wild herbs, which included walking around on the land. I also signed up to go on a week-long pilgrimage to the cave of Mary Magdalene later in the fall. I was determined to beat this thing.

The Descent. Pretend everything was just the same and barrel on. I was leading online ceremonies and seeing many clients. Even when our beautiful Samoyed puppy, who had just turned three years old, started showing signs of deep hip pain, I did not stop but instead went into overdrive to help her. It was perhaps around Beltane or early May of 2024, when I finally realized I needed to start letting things go.

About that time, my younger brother called me from Japan and told me he had been diagnosed with a terrible form of cancer. It was his third cancer. Suddenly, I could not keep all those plates spinning in the air. The first thing to go was the online ceremonies. Letting go of the crown or the headdress of the priestess: my public persona identity. Letting go of the lapis beads around the throat: my way of communicating the gifts I receive from the Goddess is through teachings and guiding others through mystical journeys inward, using my voice. Stepping away from teaching, I returned to Japan in the height of summer, with its suffocating humidity and heat, to be with my brothers. I felt the tenderness and tenuousness of my connections with family, with my birthland. There was so much I had assumed would always be the same, and yet, suddenly, I realized decades had passed and I was becoming a stranger to my own land of birth.

I let go of who I thought I was—sister to my two brothers, a daughter to my parents, both gone, a renegade daughter of the land of Japan. I saw how much distance we keep between us in our family. I started to look at how much distance I maintain from others. Letting go of the breastplate took a really long time. How to connect without fear? How to connect from a simple place of gratitude and love? How to connect without judgment? Instead of the golden breastplate simply being the symbol of the courageous warrior, I started to see it also in terms of how much it was protecting and blocking my heart.

Little by little, I began to see that I had constructed a whole identity and cosmology based on a false understanding when I was just a tiny little baby. I remember my parents looking at me with such love and fascination in their eyes as I lay in my little crib. I reached up and made a sound. I wanted to let them know I was hungry. Nothing happened. They just kept on looking at me, saying how cute I was. That's when the realization hit me that on this planet Earth, no telepathic capacity existed even when there was love. I remember this "understanding" sinking like a lead weight into the center of my being. *"This is going to be hard,"* I thought anxiously.

At the time, I still remembered the world I had just come from, where love and telepathy co-existed harmoniously. It did not help that my mother and I were such different personalities. As I grew older, she became more and more desperate to keep me safe, according to how she saw the world, negating my adventurous tendencies and criticizing me relentlessly when I strayed from her ways. My understanding that the world was a hostile place full of people wanting love and not being able to communicate became even more established.

By the time I got to the Mary Magdalene retreat in Southern France and after scrambling and slipping up a steep and rocky slope to the Womb Cave of the Magdalene, hidden high up in the mountains, I no longer really knew who I was or what I really believed in. In the depth of that prehistoric Womb Cave, held by Earth Mother and the many women who had found their way somehow into this Divine Feminine mysterium, I felt myself coming undone. Deep in the shadow realm, deep in the descent, in the Underworld, something had to be seen, let go, and a new Life reclaimed. Inanna hung dead on the meat hook for three days before she was resuscitated by the life regenerating help from the God of Wisdom, Enki.

I felt myself being hung up and still refusing to die. My mind was too strong. Great Mother, please release me, I prayed. And prayed. Let me not be the one who identifies with how she was misunderstood, how she was wronged, how she was betrayed, how good she is, how bad she is, how she was mistreated, unseen, and unheard. I don't want to be a victim. Let me become nothing, let all my ego needs disintegrate into dust.

We pilgrimaged up to the Cave three days in a row to sit in Her darkness for hours at a time. On the third day, in the depths of the dark Womb Cave, as we chanted and swayed, She seeded something into my womb. A seed of light.

Inanna is saved from Her death and brought back by two unassuming beings sent by the God of Wisdom, Enki. These beings were made from the dirt under Enki's nails, and so insignificant that they were able to slip into the Underworld realm unnoticed. There, they find Ereshkigal in the throes of birthing pain. They get down on their little hands and feet and go through the pain with Ereshkigal, groaning with Her and being right there with Her in compassion and attention. She is so moved by being seen and held in ways She never had been before, that She grants them any wish. They ask for Inanna's body, which is granted. Then these little beings successfully resuscitate Inanna per Enki's instructions and accompany Her back up, in Her ascent.

My shadow self is rebirthing herself, and I realize what she/I need is deep compassion and spaciousness. In order to give her my full attention, I am invited to let go of my previously held ways of being, seeing, and understanding who I am and how I am with the world.

This death/rebirth process for me is gradual, and I am learning to let go of my anger. I am enraged about my self-imposed armor of "protection," and the accompanying impatience and desire to control my environment. I am letting go of deep grief around self-imposed exile and separation. I am even letting go of a goal. I don't know exactly where I am going or where I am being led. It is opening up a whole area of trusting and surrendering. My intention is to heal and expand beyond who and where I think I am or want to be. Then I am giving up all notions of how and what that would even look like.

There is huge grace in this unfolding as I am starting to wake up each day with more gratitude and peace. I have been guided to resume my Reiki training and practice after an almost twenty-year hiatus and am now a Reiki Master. This is helping me open in a new way to how I give and receive healing from and with the forest I live in. I feel less afraid and separate, and live more in gratitude and opening to love. A little more surrendered. A little softer . . . and less annoyed by little and big things out of my control.

In this liminal space where I am right now, in between the shape of what has been, and the creation/manifestation of what is to come,

I often see the image of Kuan Yin, the Goddess of Healing and Mercy, riding the Water Dragon. The Dragon is fierce and wild, while She stands upon the Dragon's back, so at ease, balanced, full of grace, and peaceful. It helps me to bring myself back, over and over again throughout the day, to be compassionate and grateful, loving and at peace, even as I ride the wild, Life energy of living on this Planet Earth.

Below is my own, modified version of the Reiki prayer, which helps me. I offer this to my fellow travelers on the path. May it smooth the wild ride of this Life for you, as you ride your Dragon. Blessed Be.

Today, I let go of my anger.
Today, I let go of anxiety and grief.
Today, I am grateful for everything.
Today, I enter into respectful relationship with All Beings.
Today, I choose to abide in Peace and Love.

"I saw how much distance we keep between us in our family. I started to look at how much distance I maintain from others."

25
OVERWHELMING PEACE

Rev. Annie Bachelder

In 2019, I signed up for a writing class. Half-heartedly, I hoped to learn to write compelling marketing copy for my services as an Akashic Channel. During the first session, experienced students read passages of their writing, and the instructor gave feedback. During the second session, the instructor led us in a brief consciousness preparation process. Like a shot, I began to write.

Without giving it a thought, I began channeling the Akashic Beings of Light and their introduction to *Bringing Forth Soul Consciousness*. Prior to that moment, I had not one whit of a desire to write a book. I had not been told by any of my spirit guides that I was to write a book, especially not one that involved deeply esoteric principles that were somewhat above my pay grade. Every time I sat down to write, I received another channeled transmission for the book. Many times, when I began to write, the Akashic Beings of Light had to "handle my case." By that I mean these loving Beings of Light had to calm my emotions and focus my scattered thoughts so I could channel their energy and information for *Bringing Forth Soul Consciousness*. This accounts for the meditative quality and content of many chapters. Chapter 28 is an excellent example of this. It is also why there are 13 guided exercises that teach energy skills and ways of working purposefully in the Akashic Records. Years later, I continue to enjoy and incorporate the principles of this material.

Most morning meditations include opening my Akashic Records with the prayer at the beginning of Chapter 28, communing with my Soul, the Akashic Being of Light, and the Great Creatress. This is the name of the supreme Divine feminine used by the Akashic Beings of Light. I also use the technique of embodying my Soul's Light and Consciousness many times a day. The process happens instantaneously now. It consistently smooths my emotions and clears my thinking. I treasure the added experience of being completely enveloped by the Great Creatress. I picture myself filled with my Soul's Light, surrounded by the Great Creatress, feeling unconditionally confident. I observe what I want to experience, and the resources I need, simply arrive. Fear transforms into stillness. Resentments vanish. I feel alive, on purpose, and know what to do, or not do. I know when the energy is ripe for action and when it is not. I trust my Soul and the Great Creatress. I feel spiritually aligned and ready to be of service to students, clients, and others as we navigate our Soul's Divine plans. Truly, the Divine doeth the works. Not I.

I hope that the readers of the chapter below sense, and benefit from, the energy in it. I hope readers, and those they share it with, find it equally effective and helpful as it has been for me.

Chapter 28 Overwhelming Peace
Channeled by the Akashic Beings of Light

Akashic Records Prayer ~ Opening Prayer:

1. By the Power of Divine Light within me
2. Come Holy Spirit! Spirit of Light! Spirit of Truth!
3. For the highest good of all, throughout time, fill my heart with Divine Love as

4. I humbly ask permission to open the Divine portal to the highest realm of the Akashic Records for (LEGAL NAME).
5. Akashic Beings of Light, guide me to the deepest Truth of my being, releasing any blocks & restrictions to my abundance & highest good.
6. Great Creatress, assist me to fully embody my Soul's Light, to fulfill my Soul's purposes, & to heal any accumulated karma.
7. Surround me with the enlightenment & wisdom of my Masters, Teachers, & Loved Ones.
8. Clearly direct my perspective & actions to those that manifest my Divine Plan.

(Repeat lines 5, 6, 7, & 8 two more times, then say line 9)

9. Free of all resistance, judgment, and fear, I am now filled with Divine love & the Records are now open.

Greetings and welcome from the Akashic Beings of Light.

There is no greater place to be than where you are now. Sense the ground under your feet. Sense the moment. Alive with breath and the steady beating of your heart. Since your desire is to be at one with the moment. Set aside any resistance you feel. Just BE in this moment. Acknowledge the love you have flowing through you, the tender sensations of caring about, and honoring of, your experience of this moment. Continue to breathe deeply while your shoulders relax. Simply BE for the moment. Nowhere to rush to. No transitioning from one role to another to force into place. Feel into the deep peace of the moment. This moment. Here. Now. Lean into the now moment that stretches forever outward in all directions. Release yourself from a box, a form, a role, a task, bound by doing. Feel. Breathe. Pulse. Float.

Allow yourself to place all your concerns into the hands of the Great Creatress. Let yourself float on the moment like a flower in a quiet stream, flowing peacefully onward to a distant destination. Be slow, lay low. Grant yourself the gift of this peace. Nowhere to be and nothing to do. Simply be in the stillness. Let any feelings float up to the surface. A lot of relief. A hint of sadness. Not serious or overtaking. Feelings coming and going, flavoring the moment. Release the demands you put upon yourself. Put down your walking stick. Soften your focus. Let all things that are present for you here be equal, none better or worse, none requiring action or greater attention. Breathe into the soft focus. Loosen the ties that have bound you. Ease up on pressing yourself forward. Relax. All is well. Let go of getting a jump on the next task or problem. Let others be in charge for a while. You get to be. Just be. No requirements for the moment. Revel in the peace. Stretch out in the peace. Soak it up. Absorb all you can of this peace and steadiness. Breathe it into your interior. This peace comes from within you. It always exists within you. When you abandon your cares, giving them to the Great Creatress, this peace is what arises naturally, easily, effortlessly. This peace is who you are. This peace is the ground of your being. No more and no less than any other relevant act or state of being, this peace is who you are. Revel in it. Absorb so much peace that you overflow with peace. Exude it. Radiate peace. You have plenty.

This peace is what is experienced after death. This is the reception you receive after releasing the body. Feel the natural lifting of gravity that has pulled on you for so long. The gravity that has tethered you to the planet.

Notice that even here, in this moment, you have free will to choose. You can be overwhelmed by peace or overwhelmed by doingness, or overwhelmed by love, or overwhelmed by grief and emotions. All of these options can exist within this one moment. Equally present, equally powerful, and potent. However, you, in this moment are choosing peace. Be present to this Soul quality within you. Let it restore you, calm you, cradle you in safety. Let this moment stretch on into infinity. It is the peace that offers itself to you whenever you need it. You can fall into this peace. It is yours! Embrace it as if it were your pillow. Pull it to you, shaping it to your liking, forming it to that perfect comfort you know so well. Surrender to this peace like a child innocently surrendering to sleep. Drifting off effortlessly. No thoughts. No deeds. No plans. This peace is a part of who you are, at heart, deep within.

And from this place, you experience the greater reality of your existence as a Soul, as peaceful Soul consciousness, a part of the whole of creation. Embody your Soul's Light now, while there is no fight in you, while there is nothing to force, nothing to command, nothing to oversee, nothing to manage. The details are quietly corralled for the moment. Be grateful for this delicate moment of simply being. A true Sunday morning moment. Of Peace. Of joining the Great Creatress and All That Is. Resting in the bosom of Her embrace. Look around your interior and know that all is well. All unfolds according to Her timing. Surrender and be overwhelmed by Her peace. This is the peace that surpasses all understanding. It is peace felt in the heart. Peace in the mind. The ego is silenced for a blessed moment, and it is restored to balance in this peace. No resistance. No argument to win, no point to prove. Just be. Just be. Dissolve into the breath. Dissolve into your heartbeat. No identity. No individuality. All is all. All is whole. Let this float down to the deepest part of you. Breathe it into the tip of the tailbone. Return at will. Know that you are invited to enter this expansive chamber, as often as you like. Choose it. Be it.

We bid you good day for now.

Bringing Forth Soul Consciousness
Akashic Records Closing Prayer:

1. Thanking the Great Creatress & Her Holy Spirit for Love, protection, and healing received this day,

2. Thanking the Akashic Beings of Light for guidance,

3. Thanking the Masters, Teachers, & Loved Ones for wisdom and direction.

4. The Divine Portal & the Akashic Records are now closed. Amen. Amen. Amen.

26

ME AND MAGDALENA:
Healing Holy Heretics

Shelley Lynn Hines, MSN

I came into this world knowing invisible energies even whilst still in the crib. I was told that I had terribly frightened my mother, who was raised in the Church, abused by Catholic priests, and didn't know what to make of her tiny, demon child who gleefully gurgled, laughed, and played with lighted orbs of energy in ways she couldn't understand. Some would call me especially sensitive, a natural empath, and a healer. I consider myself a Magdalene and mystic with a sharp eye for integrity and a beautiful mission with my feet in both this world and on the other side of the veil for an incarnation of varied healings and expressions.

I deeply resonate with the stories of Mary Magdalene, who is celebrated each year on July 22 for her contributions to the teachings of the Christ. In 2016, healing and hope came for me in the form of a divine download (an assignment) about the Asteroid-318~Magdalena, which features prominently in my astrological chart. Her stories, folklore, and archetypes come alive for me in their symbolism. This bright and shiny celestial Light comes to us as a messenger, just as Yeshua (Jesus) and Miryam (Magdalene) did, calling us to be free and choose our inner kingdoms of heaven, to let our voices be heard, and to honor the return of the Divine Feminine. As a pastoral Evolutionary

Astrologer (EA), this synchronicity of past and current global events is not lost on me. (EA combines psychology with archetypal astrology, and I come from a spiritual approach.)

My conscious introduction to the Divine Feminine began in the 1980s when I heard a female voice speaking to me. I was in an extremely dangerous relationship with a violent addict—a severely wounded soul (also abused by priests) who was uncomfortable with my curiosity about any religious study. To keep peace, I betrayed myself and became as one of Margaret Atwood's characters in *A Handmaid's Tale*. My moral conflict of self-erasure for survival led me to feign disbelief in Spirit—my term for Mother-Father-God.

Negotiating my inner truth with outward compliance lasted about six months. I was in physical and emotional pain. Like many women in a bad relationship, I had stayed far too long and was barely managing. One hot day, I was sitting on the living room floor of my home in a Southwestern US desert city, where my life felt like a scene from Atwood's dystopian tale of Gilead. The children were in school, he was at work, and I was not in a good way, but then magical healing came. In that quiet living room, I clearly heard a feminine voice, which wasn't mine, say to me, "Come back, Daughter!"

Naturally comforted, I excitedly and secretly unpacked the feminist books I had been reading but had hidden from him. That day, my secret affair with the books of feminist scholars and theologians grew within my heart as did my courage. Books like: *Women Who Run with the Wolves*, *When the Drummers Were Women*, *The Chalice and the Blade*, and many more steeled me for changes to come.

After hearing my call to "Come back, Daughter," I did. I came back, and I've never left. I've been a follower of the Feminine Divine ever since. In gaining my Spiritual strength, I found my voice. I finally spoke my truth (to dark power) and very carefully stood up to him.

I said, "I love you, but I don't need to be treated like this anymore." After an inconsequential parting shot, he was gone within a span of two weeks.

I continued my spiritual quest, and before long, I found the Gospel of Thomas, the Gospel of Philip, and the Gospel of Mary; ancient texts not included in the official canon of the Bible. To me, as a seeker, they were like a tantalizing mystery. I wanted to know why these texts had disappeared. When I got my first copy, reading the Gospel of Mary was one of the richest discoveries I have experienced while reading, even with much of the manuscript missing. The words informed me like whispers from the past, helping me remember the truth about what it was like to live in that era, what it was to walk with that profound mission of healing and the Good News.

Like desert sands, time drifted by with more personal growth. A move to the Pacific Northwest brought forth more healing experiences, especially around my voice. I was intrigued when, in June 2016, Pope Francis raised Mary Magdalene to a Feast Day status. I was attending a small New Thought church and asked the lead minister if I could give a special talk about Magdalene on her Feast Day, as I was already familiar with her Gospel. He was supportive and eager for me to do this and said, "Yes, this is important. Come, talk!"

You know that they say be careful what you ask for? I quickly got buyer's remorse. My unassailable seeking was bringing up buried knowledge that had been locked in my unconscious memories. Without warning, I started having a string of past life recollections and flashes of knowing where I was shown where my voice had been violated, silenced, and worse. It was upsetting to say the least. To calm myself, I did breathwork techniques that I learned as a past-life hypnotherapist and certified nurse-midwife. I got settled, and my body calmed. In that moment of self-healing, I heard that mystical guide's voice again instructing me to, "Look up the Asteroid Magdalena."

As an experienced Master Evolutionary Astrologer, I had never heard of this one. I opened my computer to search, and sure enough, I found Her! The magic of this moment was that the voice I heard was quite explicit in its directive. *"Look up the Asteroid Magdalena,"* not Mary or Mother Mary or Mary Magdalene! I still get 'truth-bumps' every time I tell this story, which indicates to me that I need to keep sharing it.

Asteroid data was placed into my computer; I pulled up the chart to find more enchantments. The discovery chart for the date the asteroid was discovered shows that indeed, Her signature is one of being a message bearer, teacher, healer, and so much more. A bonus and my admitted bias is that she holds a position in the first house of my natal chart. In non-astro speak, a planetary body in the first house is significantly difficult to deny because the first house holds the "I AM" signature.

I did not figure out right away that the astrological, archetypal expression for Her energy was that of a messenger. But now that I do, I'm leaning into it. It makes sense to me, and I know that this is something that needs to be talked about and taught in these times of awakening heretics.

Mary Magdalene was a holy heretic, a sacred messenger, and a companion or mirror to the Christ energy. That Yeshua and Miryam (my preferred names for them) go together is easy to see with a little research. Whole villages in Europe were claimed to be heretical by more than one *unholy* Pope and burned for their beliefs that these two messengers were equal companions and beloveds.

In the Aramaic language that Yeshua spoke, he used the word "Abwoon" in prayer to address God. It combines the concepts of "father" and "mother" and is derived from 'abba' (father) and 'woon' (womb). This signifies a merging of masculine and feminine principles, which is in part what Yeshua and Magdalene came to teach. We have lost much in mistranslations. Can you imagine a world where we had a holy family with a holy mother at the side of the holy Father? You know, the Great Mother-God in us all, and just as present as the Father-God. I'm a student of the Christ consciousness, the Buddha consciousness, the Magdalene consciousness. The message from Magdalena is that she was there, too, and she's here now, as well.

In future years, generations will learn about this significant period of restoration, healing, and hope that accompanies the great re-awakening to the Feminine Divine. Today, some folks are calling it a 'return,' but in my humble opinion and personal experience, the Goddess never left—she has been with me always and more recently in the form of Mary Magdalene. Currently, Magdalene's healing message of hope for the world is that we all need a Mother-God. If we had a Mother Goddess in our churches, a figurehead who is more than a virgin-mother or a woman called whore, things would be so different.

Until recently, those two were the only options, and call me a heretic, but we *need* the Goddess to be able to pray to, to seek solace from, to have communion with. We need more than a Virgin Mother, because that's fine and serves a purpose, but it's not enough.

If those ancient gospels had not been destroyed or buried in the sand for two millennia, we would have a better understanding of the history and teachings of that time. Access to the Feminine Divine via Magdalene is about having a voice. One of the biggest keys to the feminine experience is to be heard and to have a place of equality. If Mary Magdalene was the Lighted mirror reflection of the Christ, then you can't have one without the other. Just as the moon reflects the sun's light back to itself. Once this feminine wound is healed within each of us (men and women), then it is a gift that we're able to give back to the collective.

In some of my past lives, I had a powerful voice. Many in authority did not agree with my messages and silenced me. Today, that karma shows up in my relationships, home, work, and community. It is directly linked to having heretical things to say and do. Again! So, I proudly claim my holy heretic place in the universe. The word Heretic comes from the Greek *'to choose'* and to be at choice means we are free. Free to choose, free to have a voice.

In this lifetime, I am learning to soften the messages I carry. Some days I succeed and some not so much, but I am always evolving. One method I use now for expressing my voice, healing, and activism is with writing and painting with Intentional Creativity© techniques. Painting on canvas becomes a ritual and prayer (no experience is required). As I paint, I meditate, and it quiets my busy mind. It's all about getting stuff out of my head and onto the canvas. Putting brush to canvas, I enter a flow state, and the painting becomes a sacred portal through which I connect to the inner wisdom of my heart. I don't need to engage my intellect to access that state. Sometimes it's better to bypass the intellect so that the art and sacred symbolism come through more purely. I am more present, open, and receptive. I also have noticed a decrease in physical pain when in that flow state.

Our current historical and global acknowledgment of the resurrection energies of feminine healing and hope, directly tied to the Magdalene, is coming through so strongly now. The rise of collective consciousness around Mary Magdalene is blossoming across books, theatre, song, and film—restoring her as a symbol of sacred feminine wisdom and spiritual leadership. As her story resurfaces, discernment is vital, for she and we are healing holy heretics reclaiming our voices in a time finally safe for truth. Where does Magdalena hold potential power in your life? Discover it, heal, and then come join me and the rest of us holy heretics. We are free to choose!

27
HUMANITY'S DESTINY

Channelled by Zaher Kury
excerpted from *The Evolution Revolution*

My name is the Evolution Revolution. I am an energy projection of the universal consciousness and its creation. I am here to bring to you a conscious realization about your destiny, the explanation of how humankind's God is the Universal Consciousness Energy. If everything is energy, then God must be, also.

This knowledge is not new to you. Only the words have changed. This consciousness energy has been working with humanity for thousands of years and beyond, to bring energetic balance to humankind. That time has arrived.

I am speaking for myself because my energy is unlimited in its ability to create. As an energy, I was transformed into physical thought, and from there I became words. What am I saying, you ask? How could it be that a consciousness energy is actually your God? It's not easy to explain this energy using man-made words. Simply put, Energy is Energy.

How can there be consciousness beyond the brain? Consciousness energy creates the brain, and it uses physical energy to run it. Do you believe in physical evolution? Do you know what it is? You can find answers in here. I am a book that has taken a look into humanity and realized that today's humanity is the same as yesterday's humanity. These pages will tell you why.

As a book, I take the reader on a journey from the present moment into a future where humankind will meet its destiny. When you read me, my words will help you develop a new perception, a new view of you, and the world around you. I will explain the energy movement that led to the Evolution Revolution. The intention of this revelation is to create awareness of the universal consciousness energy and its connection to humanity.

Humanity was created by this universal consciousness energy. It's an energy that constantly revolves and evolves. As it evolves, it creates. Humanity has been calling the universal consciousness, God, since the creation of religion. It was an attempt to explain the creator, and it failed. It had limits and no answers because the consciousness energy is unlimited in its knowledge of creation.

Since the beginning, there have been attempts at awakening humanity to the realization that the universal consciousness energy is its Creator. Every aspect of creation, even the creation of the creator, is an energy evolution.

In my pages, you will discover the What, When, Where, Who, and Why of the universal consciousness. You will meet personalities who have learned about it, as well as those who are still learning. I am not just a book. I am humanity's reflection; all parts, the good and bad. You are aware enough to know what's around you, but are you aware of your creator, the universal consciousness?

The words of my pages are another attempt at making contact and inspiring humankind to take action. You have your own perception, this is true, but don't let your perception keep you from learning something new. Otherwise, your perception is limited and has an ending. What is being presented to you is about your Past, Present, and Future. What you can do is share me with your family and friends.

You are going to read about the perception of the Earth, as she reacts to humanity's treatment of her. These words are meant to reach you and your perception, to make you aware that life never ends. You will also learn from those who participated in the Evolution Revolution and their stories of transformation.

You will read about the comparison between the universal consciousness and God. Religion has something to say. But then, so does humankind. I am an open book until you close me. But if you close me, you will miss an important link. It's hiding in the shadows, waiting for you to find it.

In these pages, you will hear from the participants of the energy movement and the physical Evolution Revolution themselves, speak about their experiences with their own energy conversion, and how they started the energy movement.

I am a book that has come to bring to you an ability to make choices. I have come to reach you, not to preach to you. I brought you a conversation with the Universal Consciousness Energy. My suggestion is that you read all of me.

I am full of ideas that you have thought of before but did not act on. This knowledge will change you, just as it gave me my voice. It will empower you to find your voice again. You will learn to recognize the power inside you that wants to be unleashed, that wants to change, that wants to grow in consciousness. It will give you the power to face all your fears.

Nothing is as it seems when it comes to humanity's actions. You may think that you know the issues, but to only know creates nothing until what you know creates change. To understand me is to read me.

Your story begins in the present day. The future will tell the rest of the story. The future is not there waiting for you.

Let this be your bridge to creating it. When you reflect on what you read, use consciousness energy as your guide. What you do with this knowledge is your choice, as long as you are making your own decisions. You will develop your own impressions.

ABOUT OUR AUTHORS

YUKIKO AMAYA

Yukiko Amaya is a healer, yogini, sacred temple dancer, shamanic practitioner, writer, Reiki Master, and Priestess of Avalon. She is passionate about restoring our broken relationship with Earth, Nature, and all beings, which in turn mirrors our broken relationship with ourselves. This Way of circular relationship and respect for each other as well as ourselves, she calls the Goddess Path or the Way of the Divine Feminine. Her healing work, rituals, teachings, and sacred immersions come out of her own life experiences, studies with teachers and mentors of various traditions, and guidance from Source. She is currently on a sabbatical year exploring the Path of Love of Mary Magdalene and Yeshua, or the marriage of the Divine Feminine and Divine Masculine.

She lives in the mountains surrounding the Shenandoah Valley of Northern Virginia with her husband and their Samoyed puppy and fluffy cat.

As a writer, she is working in the vein of the Literature of Restoration, i.e. restoring our relationship with Nature and each other through literature. Excerpts of her current work in progress can be seen at www.literatureofrestoration.org/untitled-yukiko-amaya/

Find Yukiko online:
www.MyGoddessPath.com
www.youtube.com/@mygoddesspath469
www.Instagram.com/yukikoamaya

REV. ANNIE BACHELDER

Reverend Annie Bachelder has more than 36 years of experience as a gifted channel, psychic, medium, and spiritual teacher. Annie's natural psychic abilities have been further refined through practicing and teaching many workshops, including Awakening Your Light Body, Opening to Channel, How to Read the Akashic Records, Living as Your Soul Writing Workshop, and Healing Self-Doubt.

Despite overcoming personal challenges, including healing her disability due to multiple sclerosis, a miscarriage, three tubal pregnancies, and painful adoption experiences, Annie channeled the transformative book Bringing Forth Soul Consciousness, offering 13 Akashic Records-based guided exercises and energy skills to help you live a Soul fulfilled life. Her daily practice of embodying her Soul's Light guides her in serving students and clients, providing greater calm, confidence, and clarity through Akashic Records Readings and empowering others to explore their own Records with depth and ease.

Find Annie online:
www.anniechannels.com
www.soulsourcer.etsy.com
facebook.com/annie.bachelder
www.youtube.com/channel/UCkI8K0gm24Hh4ibfD6_WW3Q

SANDRA BARGMAN

Sandra Bargman is a creative soul, an intuitive communicator, and servant leader. She is a contributing author to the best-selling book, *On the Shoulders of Mighty Women* by Lesley Michaels, with her chapter, "Anger and the Reluctant Leader." She has been a featured writer at OPAL Magazine and MaximizeU.Life, and on many wellness websites.

Sandra is a 35+ year professional actor/singer/voice actor (AEA/SAG/AFTRA), holding a BFA from Carnegie Mellon University. She is a seminary-trained and ordained Interfaith Minister, award-winning ceremonialist, and spiritual counselor. Combining actor skills with spiritual intelligence and mindfulness techniques, Sandra teaches clients ways to get comfortable and confident in their own skin for greater presence, more impactful communication, and gutsier storytelling.

Based on her award-nominated solo show of the same name, Sandra is the host of the popular podcast, The Edge of Everyday, streaming on your favorite podcast platforms and at MaximizeU.Life.

Find Sandra online:
www.SandraBargman.com
Instagram: @SandraBargman
#TheEdgeofEverydayPodcast

SHEHERAZAD BARNES

Sheherazad Barnes is a devoted spiritual guide, healer, and priestess of the sacred rose lineage of Isis, Mother Mary, and Mary Magdalene. As the author of the Awakening the Goddess Within oracle cards, she channels the wisdom of these divine feminine archetypes to guide women on a profound journey of remembrance—helping them reclaim their sacred power, intuition, and sovereignty. Through her work, she bridges the mystical with the practical, offering powerful transmissions, rituals, and sacred teachings that illuminate the path of the modern priestess.

With a lifetime dedicated to service, prayer, and devotion, Shehera has cultivated a deep connection to the goddess and the ancient mysteries. Her teachings blend channeled activations, sound healing, goddess archetypes, alchemical practices, and ancient Egyptian wisdom. These gifts help to heal the feminine nervous system, activate spiritual gifts, and restore harmony between the cosmic and earthly realms. Drawing from initiatory lineages, she creates transformational spaces for women to heal generational wounds, embody their highest soul expression, and step into their divine mission with clarity and power.

Find Sheherezad online:

www.anahataholistichealing.com
www.instagram.com/iamsheherazad
www.facebook.com/shehera

JENNIFER COFFEY

Jennifer Coffey is a sacred space holder for transformation—a Co-Active® coach, writer, and Movement Medicine® Apprentice Facilitator. Fascinated by the sacred weave of mind, movement, story, and spirit, she follows the thread of healing, depth, and mystery wherever it leads.

Though she has no children of her own, she is a spirit mother to many and the lucky steward of a four-legged beam of love in dog form. She is honored to coach other coaches as they refine and embody their unique blend of gifts, and welcomes invitations to facilitate curated groups in private, corporate, and retreat settings.

Find Jen online:
jencoffey@gmail.com
www.jencoffeycoaching.com

Photo credit: Stephanie Mohan, Creative Portraiture

CEARA FATE

As a multidimensional creative and spiritual practitioner, Ceara Fate walks the line between sound, soul, and systems. As a writer, intuitive, expressive vocalist, and online business manager, her work explores the tension between digital connection and human disconnection, creating both sonic and sacred spaces for emotional truth and energetic healing. Her experiences growing up online have shaped a unique lens on the modern myth of "always-on" culture, inspiring her to question what it really means to be present, seen, and whole.

She is the founder of Fateful Awakening, a space for psychic healing and spiritual reconnection, and Bleeding Rose Creative, where she supports heart-led entrepreneurs in building sustainable, soul-aligned businesses. Through all of her work, she holds space for those who feel too much and still want more.

Find Ceara online:
www.cearafate.com
www.linkedin.com/in/cearac/

KEN HAROOTUNIAN

Ken Harootunian has had a long career in nonprofit management, strategy, and development. He has been a leading development professional for numerous organizations, including Planned Parenthood (three times), Stanford University's School of Engineering, The Wharton School of the University of Pennsylvania, the East Bay Community Foundation, HomeRise, and the Institute for the Future.

He now serves as Chief Development Officer at TLC Child & Family Services of Sonoma County, serving 600+ clients, including foster kids, foster families, and housing at-risk young adults who are runaways or have timed out of the foster care program. He also serves on the board of two nonprofits: the Numi Foundation and is the Board Chair of Exposing Hope.

Find Ken online:
www.tlc4kids.org

SHELLY LYNN HINES, MSN

Shelley Lynn Hines is a Registered Nurse, Pastoral Evolutionary Astrologer, and Intentional Creativity® teacher whose calling is devoted to soul healing, empowering women through remembrance, and awakening the Divine Feminine. With more than three decades of experience, she bridges science and mysticism to support U.S. and International clients in reclaiming their wellness and divine purpose.

Her unique approach blends mindfulness, astrology, and creative ritual to illuminate each soul's karmic path and purpose. Her work involves the once hidden sacred teachings of Mary Magdalene and includes the powerful influence of the asteroid Magdalena. Bringing a revolutionary lens to modern astrology, she is helping clients unlock the codes of inner sovereignty and embodied mysticism.

During her signature *She Rises in Wellness Women's Retreats*© and personalized one-on-one sessions, Shelley creates sacred spaces for healing, awakening, and creative expression, where each woman is invited to rise into her sovereignty, wisdom, and truth. Her mission is clear: to help others remember who they truly are and rise in wellness.

Find Shelley online:
www.shelleyhines.com
astrologyshines@gmail.com

LORENZO JONES

As an executive business coach, speaker, facilitator, and trainer, Lorenzo focuses on fostering productive learning environments and establishing trust-based relationships with clients and community benefit corporations. Lorenzo has worked with individuals and organizations across the US, collaborating with executives, board members, and teams to support their goals.

As an inspirational leader, Lorenzo emphasizes the importance of overcoming limiting beliefs. He communicates in a manner intended to engage and motivate clients and supports them in identifying barriers and exploring new perspectives. His interest in talent development was inspired by his own personal development journey and working alongside mentors, including assisting with projects in Ghana.

Influences in Lorenzo's life include his grandparents, his great-grandfather's entrepreneurial activities, and his mother's commitment to her work and family. Originally from the Midwest, he relocated to California to pursue his education. Personal interests include hosting informal dinners at home, drumming, cycling, and traveling, with aspirations to experience an African safari.

Find Lorenzo online:
www.linkedIn.com/in/lorenzojones

LEAH KAHN

Leah Kahn has trained hundreds of educators and rabbis in the art of teaching. She is currently the Vice President of Education at Assembly, and prior to that held a 14-year career in Hillel, both on campus (Berkeley Hillel/UChicago) and nationally. Over the course of her career, she has designed many curricula that have supported hundreds of educators and impacted thousands of learners. She has taught at the Wexner Institute, Mechon Hadar, the Pardes Institute of Jewish Studies, and Hillel International, among others. She is currently adjunct faculty at the Academy of Jewish Religion.

Leah has an MA in Jewish Studies and Experiential Education from the Spertus Institute and a certificate in Jewish Studies from Pardes. She was awarded the 2016 Pomegranate Prize (Covenant Foundation), received the 2018 Fromer Award in Arts and Education (East Bay Federation) for her choreography, and was a senior fellow in the M2 Pedagogies Research Fellowship (2020). She is currently a Wexner Field Fellow in Class 8, has three yoga certifications, and holds an undergraduate degree in Dance Performance from Columbia College Chicago. Leah is a lifelong modern dancer, Shabbat enthusiast, and a mean vegan cook. At camp, she will be teaching Jewish learning classes, leading a yoga seder, and teaching yoga classes. She lives in Chicago with her husband and two kids.

Find Leah online:
leah@assembly.community
www.assembly.community

CATHERINE KAUFER

Catherine Kaufer is a published author, Transition Expert, and Minister dedicated to guiding women through life's most challenging transitions. She is the host of Embracing Life Again, a transformative TV show offering practical tools, heartfelt stories, and faith-based guidance to help women rediscover joy and dream again.

With her registered therapy animals and certification in Healing Trauma through Horses (Faith-Based Equine Assisted Philosophy™), Catherine integrates the profound healing power of animals into her work. At Redeemer Ranch in Reno, Nevada, she hosts community gatherings, retreats, and one-on-one therapy sessions, creating a safe and sacred space for personal growth and renewal.

DEE DEE KIESOW

Dee Dee Kiesow is an award-winning fundraiser, consultant, speaker, and former corporate sales executive with 30+ years of leadership across nonprofit and for-profit sectors. She has coached and conducted more than 200 benefit auctions, helping organizations raise more than $70 million, and has served as a board member, founder, major gifts officer, CEO, and executive director.

Her resilience runs deep: after foster care, she was adopted at age 10, worked her way through college, and vowed at graduation to one day put her children through college—a promise she kept. A fourth-generation San José native, Dee Dee holds a B.A. in Radio/TV Journalism from San José State University and is bilingual in Spanish.

Through workshops, keynotes, and collaborative coaching for boards, staff, and executive teams, she designs bespoke, "learn-by-doing" programs that build skills, confidence, and measurable results. Her first book, *Fundraising in the Post-Pandemic World*, equips organizations to thrive amid uncertainty. Her forthcoming book, *Raise a Million Dollars Without Asking for a Dime*, offers a fresh mindset for joyful fundraising and donor acquisition. She has been named "Outstanding Fundraising Professional" by the Association of Fundraising Professionals, Silicon Valley Chapter.

Find Dee Dee online:
www.linkedin.com/in/deedeekiesow/

DEANA KITAJIMA

Inspired by Frank Lloyd Wright's belief that "Some people look for a beautiful place, and others make a place beautiful." As a former early childhood educator and a regional director for a private school, Deana dedicated her life to crafting nurturing spaces—both physical and metaphorical—that evoke beauty, understanding, and tranquility. This passion for creating nurturing environments extends to her design work, from imaginative play spaces to the distinct recreational and restorative areas in her private hillside sanctuary.

In early adulthood and after struggling in school, Deana was diagnosed with dyslexia and dyscalculia, which reshaped her understanding of her own abilities. Now, she channels her lived experience into advocating for neurodivergent individuals, including holding an active board position with the College of Adaptive Arts in Saratoga, CA. Deana believes that love is contagious and that if you love yourself, you can't help but love others.

ZAHER KURY

Zaher Kury was born in a small village outside Jerusalem called Birzeit. In 1967, when he was ten years old, his family moved to the United States and settled in Castro Valley, California. It was a very difficult transition for him. He was drawn to the subject of life after death, and this interest led him to focus on physical, spiritual, and mental development. With this awareness, he developed the mediumship of automatic writing and drawing, which led to the book called *From A Gun To A Flower* (1985). He has spent the last forty years developing and growing emotionally, spiritually, and consciously. He recently channeled the *Evolution Revolution, a* book that offers an urgent call to reconnect with the Universal Consciousness. It's about self-discovery, growth, and a connection with the self and its creator.

Find Zaher online:

www.Zaher.com

LISA MARTIN NAIMI

Lisa Martin Naimi is the channel and guide of *The Ascended Mastery Pathway*. Lisa serves women Healers, Energy Workers, & Yoginis to access the blueprint of their authentic expression and evolve into their calling. For 16 years, she has offered energy healing, intuitive services, psychic classes, rituals, and activations. Through her guidance, she empowers her clients to open to their Ascended Master aspect and embody those archetypal qualities for their growth and the benefit of humanity.

Lisa is certified as an Intentional Creativity Teacher with Maestra Shiloh Sophia McCloud. As an artist, Lisa paints images inspired by her Soul, Divine Feminine Ascended Masters and goddesses, and positive, life-affirming images of the feminine and their animal allies.

She now feathers her nest in Meridian, ID, with her husband, Sayed, and their lovely cat, Yoda. Lisa loves to travel, paint, write, and read research books on ancient temples and sacred sites, mystery schools, goddess cultures, future human potential, and expanding consciousness.

Find Lisa online:
www.LisaMartinNaimi.com
www.Naimiartgallery.com
Instagram: @lisa.martinnaimi

LILLY MELGAR

Emmy-nominated actress and multi-Emmy-winning producer, Lilly Melgar first came onto the entertainment scene as a VJ for Univision's "Tu Musica." A few years later, she and Ricky Martin made history as the first Latin leading couple on daytime television. After years on daytime, Melgar launched into acting in films, directing video content for major concert tours and producing.

Lilly's directorial debut was the opening video for "The Spice Girls Reunion Tour," after which she was involved, most notably, in short videos played throughout the "Britney Spears Live: The Femme Fatale Tour" and others for the "Madonna: Rebel Heart Tour."

Currently, she can be seen in the travel show, "The Wanderer," on Prime.

SARAH OLIVIERI

Sarah Olivieri is a strategic advisor to fast-growing service-based organizations and visionary CEOs who are ready to delegate their outcomes and seeking rhythm, structure, and room to lead spaciously. With over two decades of experience, she has helped leaders untangle complexity and build both strategic and operational clarity, especially within nonprofit organizations, where strategy, teams, and impact collide in uniquely challenging ways.

Sarah is the creator of the Impact Method®, a strategic framework designed to align vision, leadership, and execution, and host of the top-rated podcast Inspired Nonprofit Leadership.

She believes success isn't about doing more, it's about choosing what matters. And when you define that clearly, you can build wildly profitable businesses and financially free nonprofits that support your life, instead of consuming it.

Sarah has a degree in International Studies from the University of Chicago and a Master's in Humanistic Multicultural Education. She's also mom to a neuro-spicy pre-teen, lover of good food, allergic to gluten, and an avid sailboat racer.

Find Sarah online:
www.saraholivieri.com

ANA MERCEDES RIVERA-PAGAN

Ana Rivera-Pagan made a career of developing people and transforming organizations. In the public and private sectors, she helped employers create values-based organizations that serve communities and nurture employees. In this work, she made powerful use of her personal story to inspire change and serve the greater good.

She's writing a memoir of her years growing up in Brooklyn after World War II, when the neighborhood was peopled with Holocaust survivors, mobsters, and a loving extended Puerto Rican family. The book is entitled, *The Bookie's Daughter.*

BRANDON PEACOCK

On June 29th, 2020, Brandon Peacock survived being shot three times in a near-fatal drive-by shooting. He was given a 50/50 chance of survival and faced the very real possibility of losing a leg. Refusing to be defined by tragedy, Brandon committed fully to recovery. He rejected pain medication, endured months of intense rehabilitation, and transformed both his body and mindset.

One year after being shot in both legs, he completed a full marathon. A few years later, he crossed the finish line of a full-distance Ironman. His journey is a powerful testament to resilience and the strength of the human spirit.

Today, Brandon is the founder of Hit The Ground Running, a mission-driven initiative inspired by those who helped him heal. He also serves as president of HealthGenie, a consulting company he runs with his mentor. With over 100,000 followers on social media, Brandon shares his story to help others find purpose in pain and strength in adversity.

His life stands as proof that even the darkest moments can lead to a future filled with meaning, growth, and impact.

Find Brandon online:
brandon@htgrcharity.com
www.htgrcharity.com
www.linkedin.com/in/brandon-peacock/

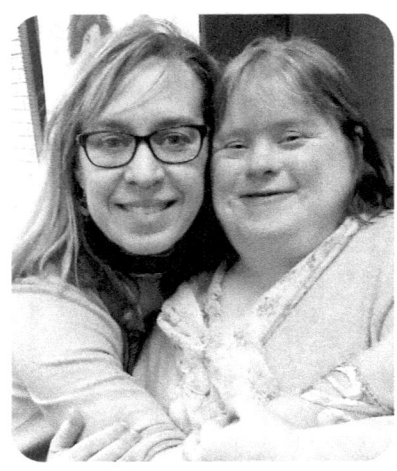

DEANNA PURSAI

DeAnna Pursai holds a Master's in Education Policy Analysis in the School of Education from the University of Illinois at Urbana-Champaign and an undergraduate degree in Elementary and Special Education from Purdue University. She is co-founder and director of community outreach of the Collect of Adaptive Arts in Saratoga, CA.

Distinctions include: Maria Shriver's Architect of Change award (2015), CNN Hero Award (2022), Boy Scouts of America Silicon Valley Character Award (2023), Women Making Herstory recipient presented by CA State Senator Dave Cortese (2023), and Golden State Warriors Impact Warriors (2024). DeAnna presented her first TEDx talk in Helsinki, Finland, on the topic of Amplifying Silent Voices (2025).

DeAnna is an active Rotarian and founded the Rotary Club of San Jose and is a co-member of the Saratoga Rotary Club. She is co-chair of the Rotary Neurodivergent Youth Empowerment Fund and serves as chair of the Rotary District 5170 Rotary Climate Action Council and vice chair for ESRAG (Environmental Sustainability Rotary Action Group) for the Big West national region. She serves as a board member of Christmas in the Park and is the beloved big sister of Angel Ellenberger, an exquisite actress, entertainer, and comedian.

TRACEY ROSE

With a B.A. in Theater Arts and a flair for the dramatic (on paper, mostly), Tracey has dabbled in writing everything from one-act plays to novels and even a self-illustrated non-fiction book. She honed her writing craft through classes with Natalie Goldberg in San Francisco and once completed NaNoWriMo, joining the elite nine thousand who finished a novel in just 30 caffeine-fueled days out of sixty thousand hopefuls.

Now living on a ranch in Northern California with her husband Jeremy, she spends her days writing, volunteering with nonprofits, and finding inspiration in everyday moments.

DR. ANNA M. VAN HEECKEREN, DVM, MS

Dr. Anna M. van Heeckeren, DVM, MS, has always believed that pets are more than animals—they're family. As a veterinarian, researcher, educator, and nonprofit leader, Dr. Anna turned this lifelong conviction into a mission: helping people and pets stay healthy and happy together. Through One Health Organization, which she founded and leads, Dr. Anna works to ensure families facing financial hardship can continue caring for their beloved companions. Her journey has been shaped by science, compassion, and lived experience—including life with Pearl, her shy rescue cat who chose Dr. Anna as her person. Whether advocating for health equity, working with other changemakers, or helping pet parents, Dr. Anna is fueled by the belief that the special connection we can have with animals makes us all better. Her work invites others to cherish these bonds and help create a world where they flourish.

To donate, visit OneHealth.org and find the Donate button or navigate to https://www.onehealth.org/donate-for-access-to-veterinary-care

As a 501(c)(3) public nonprofit registered across the US, One Health Organization is funded by people who make donations. All gifts are tax-deductible to the full extent allowed by law.

Find Anna online:
Dr.Anna@OneHealth.org
https://www.linkedin.com/in/annamvanheeckeren
OneHealth.org

RUSS WATTS + SUNNY WATTS

Russ and Sunny are partners in love, life, and adventure—and occasionally in mischief. Russ is an executive coach, facilitator, and professor who has taught leadership, health & wellness, and social entrepreneurship at Georgetown University and Bocconi University. He's also the co-founder of Story Academy, where storytelling and transformation cross paths in Italy and beyond. His career spans coaching leaders in NGOs, Fortune 50s, and global institutions.

Sunny is a teacher and experiential educator who brings creativity and play into serious learning. She's held roles at H-Farm International School, such as Experiential Education Coordinator and now full-time teacher, weaving theater, communication, and embodied practices into classrooms and workshops. She's as comfortable leading a group of international executives in Trentino and Tuscany as she is wrangling a room of curious students in Veneto—always with her signature mix of clarity, humor, and deep care.

Together, they design and facilitate transformational retreats in Italy, where leaders and seekers rediscover presence, curiosity, and joy. Their professional lives are balanced (loosely) with raising two adventurous kids, hosting long dinners that drift into late-night storytelling, and saying "yes" to improbable adventures.

Find them on LinkedIn:
www.linkedin.com/in/russwattscoachfacilitator/
www.linkedin.com/in/sunnywatts/

LEONARD WEINGARTEN

Leonard Weingarten is a seasoned marketing strategist and community engagement leader with a proven track record across the nonprofit, business, and civic sectors. Based in the Bay Area, he has successfully generated more than $500K in revenue and recruited 1,000+ members for the San Rafael Chamber of Commerce. His leadership in youth and workforce development includes initiatives that exceeded goals by 700% and earned national recognition from the U.S. Department of Labor. Leonard has raised nearly $2 million for community causes and has been honored with multiple commendations.

He managed high-profile campaigns for two Summer Olympic Games, the Rose Bowl, the Oakland Raiders, and other major events, including projects involving Ray Charles and Pope John Paul II. As a public speaker, educator, and advisory board member, Leonard shares his expertise widely, enriching both academic institutions and community organizations through his strategic insight and passionate advocacy. He currently leads continuing education efforts at the College of Marin and is a consultant to Dominican College.

Find Leonard online:
www.linkedin.com/in/leonard-weingarten

VIERA WHYE

Viera Whye is Co-Founder and has been the Producing Artistic Director for Tabia African American Theatre Ensemble and San Jose Multicultural Artists Guild since 1985. She earned her BA in Theatre and Sociology from Towson University and her MA in Theatre from San Jose State. Viera is a Director, Actor, Poet, Educator, Administrator, and HR Professional.

Viera successfully combines art and technology in her role as an Inclusion and Engagement Specialist, previously at Intel. Prior to Intel, she was a Telecommunications professional at Siemens. Her current role is Associate Director of Community Engagement at American Conservatory Theater. Viera is active in the San Jose community and a member of several organizations advocating for equity in health, education, and economic empowerment.

She has received extensive recognition and awards, most recently a Santa Clara County Lifetime Achievement Award. She was an inaugural Silicon Valley Black Legends recipient, and the Whye-Piper Arts award is presented annually in her and David Piper's name.

She is a proud mom to two handsome and witty adult sons, Copeland Bryan and Courtney Bryan.

Find Viera online:
Vierawhy15@gmail.com

DAWN AIRHART WITTE

A passionate advocate for personal growth and global change, Dawn is the author of several impactful books, including the beloved *Be...* series, which offers powerful messages of perseverance, kindness, and purpose. She brings these messages to life not only through her writing but also through her international speaking engagements and as the host of *The Secrets of Being* podcast, where she shares transformative insights on authentic living.

Dawn's deep love for humanity and animals alike is reflected in her work. She holds a certificate in Animal Assisted Therapies and Activities, which enhances her mission of bringing healing, comfort, and connection to both people and animals.

Dawn has been honored with the prestigious 2022 Presidential Lifetime Achievement Award, an Honorary Doctorate in Humanitarianism from the Global International Alliance, and the title of 2021 Women of Achievement Ms. Elite Southern California. She has served in numerous leadership roles, including PTA President, NCL-LA Founder Chapter President, and Public Works Commissioner for the City of La Cañada Flintridge.

As the visionary creator of *The Secrets of Being*, Dawn has cultivated a vibrant community dedicated to empowerment, soulful connection, and authentic self-expression.

Find Dawn online:
www.linkedin.com/in/dawn-airhart-witte-19910920/

ESTHER WYSS-FLAMM, PHD, E-RYT

Esther Wyss-Flamm, PhD, E-RYT, is a Certified Mind-Body Coach. Her former self stands in awe and surprise at how she finds herself now: a healing guide, mind-body coach, and eco-yoga instructor. She is the proud owner of White Flame Yoga in Philadelphia. She supports individuals and groups stuck at a crossroads on their path and guides them to reclaim their vitality and gifts, often in the thick of everyday family and working life.

Recently, as we witness the large and small-scale effects of climate destruction, she has been called to teach weekly in-person and virtual eco-yoga classes. These gentle movement and mindfulness practices, along with earth-based rituals, reconnect us to our natural rhythms and inner wisdom. They help creatively engage with difficult issues from a grounded place. If you feel overwhelmed and isolated by climate anxiety, this approach will help you find hope and community.

The ancient wild, wise self is always there, beckoning. When we learn to listen, events that appear to be setbacks turn into perfect, unexpected doorways into the next stage of our lives.

Find Esther online:
https://whiteflameyoga.com
ewyssflamm@gmail.com

ACKNOWLEDGEMENTS

I am grateful to my team and mentors, without whom this work would not be possible. As I am fond of saying, "When you are ready to write your book, assemble your team, and don't look back." Thank you to my lifelong pal, Nora Joanne Gerber, for your steadfast support and a forever English teacher's eagle eye. A heap of gratitude to the brilliant Ceara Costa, who holds me accountable in all the right ways. Expansive thanks to my teachers and sacred sisters, Deb Drummond, Jnana Gowan, Jessica Hadari, Christine Monaghan, and Sahar Nafal. You give my spirit and imagination wings. Of course, great reservoirs of gratitude are reserved for our LOVE NOTES community of authors who BELIEVED in the vision of LOVE NOTES, and who continue to embody the mission of LOVE NOTES every single day, leading by example, impacting their communities in elegant cosmic allemandes, spinning influence and compassion, curating connection, weaving meaning, and distilling peace. This book is made possible by the dreamers, the believers, and the magic makers, who vigilantly and everlastingly hold a greater vision for humanity and bring it to life.

WORK WITH ME!

Hi. I'm Cynthia Gregory, award-winning author and co-creative curator of the LOVE NOTES Anthologies. I believe that we are all, as Joseph Campbell phrased it—called to a hero's journey—and that the transformational stories of our lives are sourced from our souls. If you harbor a story inside you insisting on being released, I invite you to join the waitlist for LOVE NOTES 3.0 and learn more about how to step into your sacred authorship!

Schedule a free LOVE NOTES consultation call with me by visiting www.coachcynthiagregory.com

www.ingramcontent.com/pod-product-compliance
Lightning Source LLC
Chambersburg PA
CBHW052206090526
44583CB00017BA/2191